WILL POST FOR PROFIT

HOW BRANDS AND INFLUENCERS
ARE CASHING IN ON SOCIAL MEDIA

JUSTIN BLANEY, D.M.
& KATE FLEMING

Post Hill
PRESS

A POST HILL PRESS BOOK
ISBN: 978-1-64293-546-2
ISBN (eBook): 978-1-64293-547-9

Will Post for Profit:
How Brands and Influencers Are Cashing In on Social Media
© 2020 by Justin Blaney, D.M. and Kate Fleming
All Rights Reserved

Cover design by Lauren Wohlrab, Instagram.com/theartistlauren
Interior design and layout by Sarah Heneghan,
    sarah-heneghan.com

Published in association with the literary agency of Legacy, LLC, 501 N.
Orlando Avenue, Suite #313-348, Winter Park, FL 32789

Post Hill Press
New York • Nashville
posthillpress.com

Published in the United States of America

1 2 3 4 5 6 7 8 9 10

CONTENTS

NOTE

Throughout the book, there are sections directed toward either influencers or brands.

Influencer sections will have a light gray line along the left side of the paragraphs.

Brand sections will have a dark gray line along the right side of the paragraphs.

FOREWORD

OVER THE LAST DECADE I'VE PROVIDED MARKETING STRATEGY and data-driven insights for countless global brands. And while I've had the privilege of working with many talented marketers in supporting those brands, one thing has proven to be fairly consistent: marketers continue to struggle with the complex and volatile landscape that is social media. The fickle tastes of consumers are difficult to nail down. What's "lit" today will be "cancelled" tomorrow. We recognize that authenticity has to be the currency to stay relevant on social media because fake news and contrived memes have taken over feeds. Constantly changing algorithms have turned marketing on these platforms into a never-ending marathon, with brands desperately trying to keep pace.

While there is no complete antidote, the guidance shared throughout this book is a soothing balm for what ails in social-media marketing. This book unpacks the core concepts, providing step-by-step guidance in approachable language that isn't bogged down by marketing buzzwords. For example, readers are taken through the process of brand-campaign creation, and each step is articulated in just the right amount of detail—starting with defining campaign goals, establishing a budget, and choosing a media platform, and ending with identifying key performance indicators (KPIs) and secondary metrics to effectively measure the campaign's success.

Selecting the right social influencer and negotiating the terms of your relationship requires forethought and careful execution to protect the interests of the brand and the influencer. The process is not without risk, and this book's guide on how to handle that risk correctly is essential for avoiding common pitfalls. Throughout the book, the authors carefully delve into important aspects of working with a social influencer, including thoughts on budget transparency, FTC compliance, and non-compete agreements.

As a digital marketing and analytics thought leader, I've read many books that attempt to tackle the topic of social marketing but none so in depth as *Will Post for Profit*. The authors approach each aspect with a deft hand, their guidance clearly rooted in extensive experience from both sides of the work. Marketers and would-be influencers alike will benefit from reading this book and putting its concepts into practice.

Reese McGillie
Senior Director, Insights and Analytics, Tinuiti

INTRODUCTION

SINCE 2016, THE TERM *INFLUENCER* HAS BECOME ONE OF THE MOST buzzed-about terms in marketing and social media. Influencer Marketing has become an alternative option to traditional marketing channels that may be out of reach or underperforming. This is an opportunity for some brands and many influencers.

Billions of dollars in revenue are generated each year through the power of social-media influence. With the millennial generation making more than half of all their purchases online, Influencer Marketing is prime real-estate for most brands today. Influencer Marketing relies heavily on an emotional connection between the product and the advertisement. For this reason, Influencer Marketing appeals directly to the millennial and Gen Z populations.

At the most basic level, influencers are people who can cause others to change their opinions and/or actions. On the surface this sounds simple. But in terms of social marketing, it is important to understand exactly how influencers operate and how they can best be optimized. To do that, we must uncover who influencers really are and what types of influencers are out there. This book will examine what it means to be an influencer, how to become one, and how to use the influence of others to build a powerful and profitable brand.

According to the State of Influencer Marketing 2019, Benchmark Report, Influencer Marketing is still on a rapid incline and has continued to grow as an industry over the last few years, from a $1.7-billion industry in 2016 to $4.6 billion in 2018, and was projected to grow to $6.5 billion in 2019. And there has been a 1,500 percent increase in searches for "Influencer Marketing" during the same time frame.

Ninety-two percent of B2B marketers believe Influencer Marketing is an effective form of marketing, and 86 percent intend to dedicate a portion of their budget to Influencer Marketing this year—a sharp increase from 37 percent in 2017. Smart businesses that understand and follow Influencer Marketing and its trends gain up to eighteen dollars in earned media-value for every dollar spent.

There are just under 3.3 billion people worldwide (43 percent of the global population) using social media, and that number is quickly growing. While Facebook still has the largest user base, Instagram is rapidly catching up as the fastest growing social network, as of 2019. Instagram sees ninety-five million posted photos and videos each day, with over 4.2 billion likes. With Influencer Marketing as the fastest growing method for reaching customers, it makes sense to use the platforms that reach almost half of the world's population.

In many cases, YouTubers are more popular than some celebrities. This group of influencers are authentic, gaining them three times more views and twelve times more fan comments than celebrity videos. This is just one example of why Influencer Marketing is a new and exciting opportunity for many brands to increase their exposure, and also an opportunity for individuals who seek to monetize their interests on social media.

1. HISTORY OF INFLUENCER MARKETING

WHILE THE CURRENT USE OF THE TERM INFLUENCER MARKETing began in the mid-to-late 2010s, influencers have been around for hundreds, even thousands of years. In the past, these people were called prophets, philosophers, teachers, storytellers, and authors. As marketing took off in the twentieth century, brands began to make use of fictional characters to promote their products. From Coke repurposing Santa Claus into its personal mascot, to Tony the Tiger selling us frosted cereal, advertisers have long understood the power of connecting with their audiences through Influencer Marketing. Today, we call these characters Virtual Influencers. This is a new genre of Influencer Marketing, where computer-animated people recommend Maybelline lipstick, Gap apparel, and the latest Marvel movie at the cineplex.

Real people got in on the game too. The Marlboro Man and Dos Equis' Most Interesting Man in the World are examples of the kinds of influencers that can change consumer behavior and earn their respective brands untold millions in profit. As individual fame rose in the twentieth century, celebrities—whether athletes, musicians, actors, or socialites—began to cash in on their influence. For many, endorsement revenue now exceeds that of their primary source of fame.

Each of these past forms of influencers share a common trait: they all have a conflict of interest. They earned their living by promoting ideas or products. In ages past, philosophers, prophets and storytellers moved from village to village, banking on a free bed and meal in exchange for what they were selling as wisdom. They had a self-serving interest in ensuring their audience trusted what they said, regardless of their personal beliefs. Their livelihood depended upon the collection and retention of eyes and ears. Today, celebrities are selling products they don't use or perhaps even stand behind, just to collect a paycheck. Because of this, past influencers' impact has always been limited. Audiences are aware of this conflict of interest, so naturally their trust in influencers is quite limited.

The introduction of social media has generated a new marketplace of influence. In this new world, regular people have become famous for opening toys on video, revealing their daily makeup routine, or merely inviting the masses into their seemingly entertaining lives. Those who follow these influencers have a strong personal connection to them. They feel as if they know the person they are following, because in many ways they do. People today may know more about a blogger or vlogger they follow than they know about some of their own family members.

The power of today's form of Influencer Marketing is built entirely on trust. Consumers trust influencers much more than they ever trusted celebrities or animated characters. This is mainly due to influencers' relatability, which they achieve by candidly sharing their feelings and opinions, despite being paid to talk about a product. As these influencers share their daily lives and the products and services they use and love, they offer brands a unique and rich opportunity to advertise. As a result, consumers are more willing than ever to purchase what these new influencers recommend.

EXAMPLES OF INFLUENCER MARKETING CAMPAIGNS

Influencer Marketing campaigns can take nearly any form and are limited by little more than your imagination. Creating a successful campaign is discussed in greater detail in chapter 8, but here are a few successful Influencer Marketing campaigns[1] as examples.

Marriott & YouTube

Marriott was one of the first tourism brands to effectively utilize Influencer Marketing. For one campaign in particular, the hotel chain worked with YouTube influencer Jeana Smith, one half of a popular couple pranking channel (@PrankVsPrank), to celebrate reaching one million check-ins on the Marriott app. The video features a surprise dance party for the mobile user who completed the milestone check-in. The video went viral and currently has nearly four million views.

BECCA Cosmetics & Instagram

Professional model Chrissy Teigen (@chrissyteigen) is famous for her bold personality, which she shares through Instagram and Twitter. Because of her impressive following, BECCA Cosmetics collaborated with her to create a new makeup palette. Chrissy announced the new palette in an Instagram video that generated just under five million views.

---

[1]   Harley Schachter, "20 Killer Examples of Influencer Marketing," Travel Mindset, https://www.travelmindset.com/20-influencer-marketing-exam ples/.

Tom's of Maine & Micro-Influencers

Tom's of Maine (think natural deodorant and toiletries) wanted to increase brand awareness among health-conscious buyers. So, they encouraged people to try their products and share their experiences on social media. Tom's worked directly with micro-influencers, who asked their followers to publish their own posts about their experience with Tom's. This strategy created a snowball effect that reached 4.4 million potential customers in the first three months of the campaign.

Buick & Pinterest

Buick was strategizing about how to appeal to a new, younger demographic. So they asked ten design, fashion, and food bloggers to create Pinterest boards illustrating how the Buick Encore could help them express their personal style. These bloggers then published posts about the experience and promoted their boards on Facebook, Twitter, and Instagram. The "Pinboard to Dashboard" campaign drove more than seventeen million unique site-visitors.

INFLUENCER MARKETING COMPARED TO OTHER FORMS OF ADVERTISING

In many ways, Influencer Marketing is similar to other forms of brand exposure. Most advertising is simply a person or company selling access to the public's attention. The owners of real estate along a large highway can sell commuter messaging space by erecting a billboard. A TV host can be paid to promote canned chili in the middle of a segment. Someone who has gained a following on Instagram, YouTube, Pinterest, or any other social network can lease space in their feed to whomever they choose.

However, there are several key differences that can enable Influencer Marketing to provide a higher return on investment than these other forms of advertising.

Easy to Get into at Any Budget

One of the key benefits of Influencer Marketing is the ability for brands to test campaigns without significant investment. Because influencers range in audience size, cost, experience level, and ability, they can generate certain results within various contexts. A brand that focuses on building relationships and investing in small, up-and-coming influencers can benefit from the flexibility and extra effort of someone who is motivated to break into a particular market. Besides cash payment, brands can offer payment through a variety of means to entice influencers to participate in a campaign.

For example, brands can offer free product in exchange for exposure and promotional content. A company with a sizable following can pay influencers in the form of exposure to their audience by simply reposting or tagging influencers in their own posts. Brands can also negotiate better terms by offering access to valuable resources, connections, industry events, or simply the cachet of working in the industry.

In this way, a business that isn't sure if Influencer Marketing will work for it can test it on a smaller scale, then scale up its investment based on return.

Accurate Trackable Metrics

Before the introduction of digital advertising, tracking advertising campaign results was costly and largely inaccurate. Businesses might have used a custom phone number for each TV commercial or billboard to track the number of phone calls they received. They might have asked customers how they discovered their brand and hoped that enough people responded to get an accurate sample. But with digital marketing, a smart operator can create campaigns to churn out 100 percent accurate data on the results of an ad spend.

Influencer Marketing can be designed to provide this high level of accuracy, or it can be as ambiguous and inefficient as flying a blimp above the Super Bowl. This largely depends on the skill and knowledge of those executing the campaigns. Methods for setting up campaigns to provide these kinds of valuable metrics are discussed in greater detail on page 115.

Higher Level of Trust with Audience

A key benefit of Influencer Marketing is a brand's ability to leverage the high levels of trust that influencers have gained from their audience. Of course, not all influencers have the same level of trust with their audiences. However, those who do have trust are in a unique position to change the opinions and actions of thousands, or even millions, of people. They can do this on a larger scale than ever before.

Because some influencers share everything about their daily life, their audiences feel a personal connection to them. Some may even consider an influencer they follow to be like a friend or family member. Teenagers discuss the daily lives of influencers between classes. Soccer dads and moms debate every move of their favorite online personalities. Conversations around the water cooler have moved from politics and sports to social media.

Trust is the key ingredient in transferring information from one person to another. Without trust, we naturally guard ourselves. However, that guard begins to fade the more we get to know someone. Consider your reaction to meeting a stranger in a dark alley, versus meeting a friend. When new information comes from an unknown source, we treat it like a stranger in a dark alley. We pull our coats tighter. We avoid eye contact. We increase our pace. This is how consumers behave around brand messaging that comes through a channel they don't know or trust. But when that same message comes from a friend, we react differently. We lean into it. We consider it carefully. We are far more likely to act on their recommendations. The only difference is *trust*.

Influencer Marketing is built on what academics refer to as *social capital*. This is not unlike the type of capital one would typically find in a bank. It's a resource that one can use to make money, sway public opinion, or even accomplish massive public projects. Social capital is trust between people. It's the free flow of ideas and information within networks. Researchers who study this topic have found that those with more social capital are ideal candidates for disseminating ideas. This means they are connected in meaningful ways with more people, and perhaps with more well-connected people.

Traditionally, social capital has been limited to the time it takes an individual to build trusting relationships. This was only possible through personal, one-on-one interaction. Now, networks like Instagram and YouTube have broken the barriers to building social capital. These new means of communicating simulate real relationships in such an effective way that we subconsciously feel just as close to a blogger or vlogger we've never met in person as we do to people with whom we work or even live. Perhaps the most powerful benefit to marketers is that influencers are not bound by the number of hours they have in a day to network with people. They can communicate at once to millions of people. In doing so, influencers are building trust with their audience members. Each time an influencer posts, their audience gains more knowledge about them. Influencers can have millions of friends without actually spending any time with them.

Marketers can use these relationships to their advantage by paying influencers to talk about their products and services. The consumers who follow those influencers absorb these product recommendations in much the same way they would from a trusted friend. While we seemingly ignore countless marketing messages daily, we tend to listen to our friends—even if we've never met them in person.

Access to Young and Talented Storytellers

An often-overlooked benefit of working with influencers is the relatively low-cost access it can provide to young and talented storytellers who are tapped into current marketplace trends. The degree to which young people better understand the up-to-date trends of social media cannot be overstated. The latest trends, preferences, and platform uses are predominantly defined by people under the age of twenty-two. Our knowledge of the internet and social-media trends begin to deteriorate as soon as we graduate college and enter the workforce, regardless of the time we spend on social media. So working with young influencers is a great way for marketers to leverage their knowledge of social networking.

Savvy brands give these young influencers wide latitude to generate their own ideas. Although some may be vetoed, cutting-edge and profitable approaches to communicating with the next generation can emerge from these kinds of relationships. Given that influencers have already been vetted by the internet, marketers can rest assured that the influencers know how to communicate with their audience. Marketers can learn a thing or two from the influencers they hire.

INFLUENCERS ARE DIFFERENT THAN CELEBRITIES

In many ways, influencers and celebrities share similar traits. They are both known by many people. They are both paid to promote products and services. They both might even be interrupted at dinner for a picture with a fan. However, there is a key difference between influencers and celebrities when it comes to marketing. Celebrities earned their fame by doing something outside of social media. They may be a professional athlete, author, movie star, or musician. They may even have a large and engaged social following, but celebrities tend to be more private about their personal lives. They already earn millions from their claim to fame, so they are less inclined to accept money for a product they already use that might reveal something about their personal lives.

Influencers, in the context of this discussion, build their audience through social media. In most cases, they form a strong connection with their audience through sharing their daily lives. They defend their reputation by only promoting products and services they actually use and enjoy, rather than selling out to the highest bidder. Of course, this isn't always the case. Some influencers don't have a high level of trust with their audience, so it's important to discern between the two before deciding on who to work with. Plus, even if celebrities have a large social-media following, they are likely too expensive and out of reach for most brands. Even if obtaining a celebrity for a brand is within reach, it may not be advisable. The high cost of working with celebrities does not always return as good a value to the brand when compared to a group of smaller influencers who have more sway with their audience.

This isn't to say that working with celebrities is *never* a good idea, but paying for celebrity campaigns is risky and expensive, which typically means that only large brands can afford it.

TYPES OF INFLUENCERS

The term influencer has become synonymous with names like Kylie Jenner, Jeffree Star, or Shawn Johnson East. While these are influencers by their most basic definition—people who hold influence—they likely aren't the type of influencer one can just become or that companies would want to approach as a brand. In fact, there are four types of influencer and each has its own unique characteristics that make it ideal for different brands in various situations. These four categories are: content creators, makers, public figures, and virtual influencers.

Content Creators

Content creators are arguably the most sought-after type of influencer to approach as a brand or to aspire to become as an influencer. These are people who have built influence because of something they have created, something they have made from nothing. Content creators are unlike public figures who hold influence simply because of who they were prior to their social media or digital presence.

Content creators come in different forms, but they have gained influence because of something they have created on their own. They might be:

Platform-Independent Blogger/Vlogger—Someone who specializes in a certain niche, such as fashion, lifestyle, skincare, hair, etc. These content creators often share carefully thought-out updates and posts through social channels such as an online blog, vlog, Instagram, Facebook, Pinterest, etc., all with the goal of educating, promoting, or delivering something to their audience. Examples: @hellofashionblog, @gypsea_lust, @theskinnyconfidential.

YouTuber—Someone who can fit into the category of blogger but specializes in producing video content over written content. These are typically your DIY, educational, or instructional people, who value in-depth content over the static and short-text content typically found on other platforms like Instagram or Facebook. Examples: @shanedawson, @pewdiepie, @sarahsday.

Everything Else—With free reign of posting comes endless possibilities for influencer niches. This can include topics such as memes, babies or children, pets, or anything and everything else under the sun. Examples: @ kcstauffer, @fashion_laerta, @sukiicat.

Makers

Makers are another category of influencer. This may be the most niche form of influence, but at the same time, it can have a very large impact. A maker is someone who has a following based on something they created that can usually be purchased. For example, these items can be something crafty, educational, or physical. These influencers impact their community and influence the growth and direction of a particular market. Makers hold a unique position, from which they can directly push a brand that they use and that their followers would also be interested in using. Makers can transform into other forms of influencers, but their basic categories are:

Artists—They are on the edge of what is *right now*! Their following is often striving for what is next. A brand can integrate with artists to demonstrate to a large following how their product is used in real time. Examples: @anotherseattleartist, @tierrawhack, @banksy, @yanpalmer.

Brands—Cutting edge, growth focused, rule breakers who are bursting out of the box. Usually driven by filling a gap in the marketplace, these makers can often be aligned with a social or environmental purpose. They are considered the next generation of change. Examples: @scottthepainter, @pyneandsmithclothiers, @abeautifulmess.

Celebrity Makers—These makers are known for having a large social presence across social media, print, and TV. Examples: @marthastewart, @inagarten, @zacposen.

Public Figures

Public figures are generally larger accounts that belong to well-known people. They hold influence because of who they are outside the digital world. They are optimal for Influencer Marketing partnerships for brands with large budgets. Public figures, while often overlapping in categories, are:

Celebrities—Best known as actors, musicians, athletes, authors, television hosts, etc. People follow them because they've seen them in real life and want to keep up with their career or daily life. Examples: @jenniferaniston, @shawnjohnson, @taylorswift.

Skilled Professionals—Someone who has a job with a specific set of skills they like to post about. They may be dancers, chefs, artists, etc. You follow them to gain insight into their craft and to keep up with their journey. Examples: @jonboytattoo, @violetta, @stevemccurryofficial.

Models—Best known for their reputable image in high fashion, with campaigns well known across multiple, non-digital sources (print, television, runway, etc.). Examples: @gigihadid, @kendalljenner, @angelcandices.

Power Brokers—Well-known activists, politicians, etc. Examples: @ocasio2018, @gretathunberg, @janetmock.

Virtual Influencers

The latest trend in Influencer Marketing is the rise of virtual influencers. These are computer-generated characters, complete with backstories, preferences, and cheeky captions. There is considerable debate around the merits and dangers of virtual influencers. Soon, this could develop in ways we don't yet fully understand. Currently, however, virtual influencers appear to be the same as fictional characters of the past. There are several benefits to using virtual influencers, including not having to pay them. Also, they will never age, go on strike, ask for a raise, or cause a PR storm. However, virtual influencers are extensions of a brand. They are run by a committee. Their opinions are the opinions of their creators, who may have an agenda or a conflict of interest. All these factors make virtual influencers fun and novel, but nowhere near as impactful as a real person sharing their life.

Nonetheless, savvy marketers can ride the wave of interest in trends such as virtual influencers to generate a healthy return on investment. Just keep in mind that they are not the same as influencers, but are more akin to fictional, company owned, and trademarkable assets of the present and past.

Examples of virtual influencers include:

@Shudu.gram—Shudu is a digital fabrication that her creator modeled on the Princess of South Africa Barbie. She has become the jumping-off point for many virtual models across the world, influencing fashion, style, and social media.[2]

---

2   @shudu.gram, "Bio" Instagram, October 29, 2019.

@lilmiquela—Lil Miquela, who has 1.6 million Instagram followers, is a computer-generated character introduced in 2016 by a Los Angeles company backed by Silicon Valley money.[3]

@Noonoouri—Noonoouri is "cute, curious and couture and is one of the fastest growing influencers on Instagram," according to Itp.live.[4]

@Imma.gram—Imma was created in Japan by CG company ModelingCafe and was officially launched in 2018. She is so lifelike that she is often thought of as being a real person. Her images are truly uncanny, and frankly, unnerving.[5]

@Liam_Nikuro—Liam is yet another virtual influencer on Instagram. Developed by 1Sec in Japan, he focuses on popular culture and AI. Images are created by superimposing a CG head, made with the use of 3D tools, on a body filmed in live action. He is also on Twitter.[6]

Influencers can be any type or combination of public figures and content creators—essentially anyone who can harness a strong following. However, for the purposes of this book, and for understanding the details of how to become an influencer and how to utilize influencers from a brand perspective, the focus will be on content creators.

3   @lilmiquela, "Bio" Instagram, October 29, 2019.
4   @Noonoouri, "Bio," Instagram, October 29, 2019.
5   @Imma.gram, "Bio" Instagram, October 29, 2019.
6   @Liam_Nikuro, "Bio," Instagram account, October 29, 2019.

INFLUENCER SPOTLIGHT

SARAH SIMON

Artist and Author, TheMintGardener

www.themintgardener.com

Instagram: @themintgardener

Sarah Simon is the designer, artist illustrator, and author at TheMintGardener. With a continually blooming following of botanical and art lovers alike, Sarah shares her teaching talents locally in Seattle, where she regularly instructs watercolor classes to students of all skill levels.

Q: Do you want to be an influencer?

A: Even hearing that name kind of makes me go *uhhh*—I'm not 100 percent sure, but that's probably just part of my personality. My primary goal is to be an artist, but I looked it up and it defined social media influencer as a user on social media who has an established credibility in a specific industry.[7] So by that definition, I'd absolutely love that. I have an established credibility in the watercolor world, the artistic community, as well as the Instagram community. I am seen as authentic, and I am approached by a lot of brands that want me to use their product or show their product. A rule I like to follow is that I don't post about something unless I absolutely love it. If I love it, I would post about something even if I am not getting paid! In a way, I believe that helps me to be true to myself. I let people know when they reach out that if I am not a fan, and if it doesn't feel like a good

---

7   Blake Stimac, "What Is a Social Media Influencer and How to Become One," Wix Blog, May 22, 2018, https://www.wix.com/blog/2018/05/social-media-influencer.

fit for my audience, then I am not going to share about it. For example, Winsor & Newton is a fabulous brand of paint. They are hundreds of years old, from England. I have been using their paint as props in my stylings since the very beginning. They have never paid me, but they have just recently started sending me products and they are actually becoming sponsors for my book tour in 2020. On the national book tour, they have offered to create a custom set of color palettes that's going to be amazing, and basically every attendee that comes to my workshop will get this custom palette. Yes, I do want to be an influencer in a way that it establishes credibility, and I do have access to a large audience, and I do like to share with others because of the virtue of products that I believe are good for the art.

Q: What is your least favorite part about brand collaborations?

A: I feel like my least favorite part about social media or brand collaborations is that things can feel too *salesy*! It feels inauthentic. So again that's why I only like to collaborate with brands or people that I really enjoy, and that probably means that I don't make as much money with my social media as I could. But I think that my favorite part is that I can choose to engage with the people that are doing the things I support and can get behind. Sometimes brand collaborations tempt people to either go out of their genre or they tempt people with money. They think, 'Oh this looks really cool,' and then you get a lot of money, but a whole bunch of followers see that you are kind of being *salesy* or inauthentic and you lose a lot of your street credit.

Q: Is blogging your full-time job/source of income?

A: My husband is a full-time financial advisor, so that is our full-time job. For me, I'm doing this part-time. I am also a mom to two little kids. If not for all my busyness, I would probably share my YouTube to a point where I would be making more. I just don't have the time right now. So maybe one day it might be, but for now it's more part-time.

Q: What is the number-one tip or piece of advice that you would give an influencer starting out?

A: I would say you never hope harder than you work! You never dream harder than you work. I believe a lot of the work has to be done on yourself first. You need to figure out what you are interested in and pursue that. Don't quit your day job before you invest and work hard to build a platform. For example: I love to garden and I also love to paint. My husband also happens to love to garden, so that's something that was already naturally built into our lives. The mint gardener was a very natural way to transition from planting in our garden, what I love to do already, combined with my passions and interests. Sharing feels very natural, and sure, sometimes social media feels like work. I show up because that's what you do for work, but it does make the job a lot more enjoyable because I am already sharing about things that I absolutely love.

This complete interview is available in Appendix E on page 202.

AUDIENCE SIZE CATEGORIES

FOR INFLUENCERS

As influencers grow and evolve, they will reach many milestones. They will inevitably experience several changes, stigmas, and requirements. On the journey from zero to one million followers, influencers will pass through various phases. While some influencers start out as nobodies, they can grow to become nano-influencers, micro-influencers, mid-level influencers, large-level influencers, mega-influencers, and even brand-worthy influencers. If they become really successful, they may even evolve into public figures.

FOR BRANDS

Don't make the mistake of assuming bigger is always better. Yes, companies can widen their reach through influencers with millions of followers, but the cost per post will also be significantly higher. This is one of the headaches that can come from working with celebrities. On the other hand, influencers with fewer followers can provide a much better service. They may also be more likely to build a relationship that can expand as they grow. This can ultimately create a better return on investment.

Nano-Influencers (0–3K Followers)

Everyone must start somewhere. Every influencer has begun with zero followers at some point in time. This is the period when they are beginning to figure everything out. They may not have yet solidified their handle, persona, social platform, or branding. They may still be lacking attention to detail on their content (whether image, video, or text). And they may have yet to take into consideration a theme or content calendar. It's also the phase of their journey where new influencers start to realize the time, energy, and commitment that comes with running digital platforms, and they decide if the influencer life is right for them. At this point in their journey, it is unlikely that they will interest brands in collaboration. However, there are opportunities to earn money promoting brands through affiliate programs. Nano-influencers can also get discounts on items or brands they wish to promote. In some cases, they can even earn free product as long as they promote it to their audience.

Some companies may think that an Instagramer or YouTuber with 2,000 followers isn't worth their time, but don't underestimate how much can be done through an army of smaller social-media power-users. In general, the smaller the audience, the higher engagement these influencers have with their followers. Social media platforms tend to prioritize friends and family in the algorithms that generate our feeds, so these smaller influencers are more likely to reach more of their audience on a post-by-post basis. They also tend to have a higher level of trust with their audience based on geographic or emotional proximity alone. Brands can often get these nano-influencers to promote their product just by making them feel important. Companies can offer discounts or free product to nano-influencers if it fits within their business model.

When choosing which nano-influencer to work with, brands should consider more of a shotgun approach. Realistically, it's impossible to evaluate thousands of small influencers for fit. Instead, companies can set up a program that influencers can opt into. They may have a set of rules they agree to follow, and a staff person who spot-checks for compliance. When executed properly, this can be an ideal way for brands to assess this level of influencer for their marketing campaigns. In some cases, campaigns with many nano-influencers can yield a higher return on investment when compared to working with other levels of influence.

Micro-Influencers (3–20K Followers)

As an influencer's following begins to increase and they've decided this is the path they want to pursue, they will transition into the level of the micro-influencer. Micro-influencers' audiences can have either the highest or lowest impact, depending on the brand/influencer collaboration. For example, an influencer may only have 10,000 followers, but they are highly motivated to engage with the audience. This could result in a 20 percent engagement rate. At 30,000 followers, the same level of engagement is nearly unheard of. This means that even though a micro-influencer's following size may be small, brands will likely still be very interested in working with them. At this stage in audience size, the most important thing for influencers is to continue to focus on creating quality content and an engaged audience. Depending on the niche and engagement, micro-influencers might start seeing paid brand collaborations around the 4,000-follower mark.

Micro-influencers are perhaps the best opportunity for a brand to test out if Influencer Marketing is for them. There are plenty of people to work with, and for the most part they are available at affordable prices. Most micro-influencers tend to be more professional than nano-influencers. Many influencers at this level will work for free or for discounted product. There will be a handful, however, who will insist on some form of payment. Otherwise, many of the same points apply as with nano-influencers.

Mid-Level Influencers (20–100K Followers)

The sweet spot of influencer engagement is between 20,000 and 100,000 followers.[8] These might experience a slight decline in engagement over lower-level influencers, which is typical with growth, but this is the level where audience trust and credibility are usually at their highest. Mid-level influencers are still able to maintain an ideal influencer/audience relationship with this following. At this size, brands will begin to reach out more frequently for collaborations. It's important for mid-level influencers to remember their dedication to their audience and domain. Not all collaborations are good ones. Maintaining honesty and authenticity is key. By this point, influencers should have a solidified name and handle, cohesiveness among platforms, and a concrete content-calendar, which we will discuss later.

For many brands, mid-level influencers are a great way to maximize their return. Though these influencers will notice less engagement per 1,000 followers, companies can more easily scale their reach through this audience size without the complexities of working with larger-than-life personalities and other celebrity types. Brands should expect to pay for most campaigns at this level, though there is always the chance that they can offer product if the influencer wants to break into the company or industry. Mid-level influencers tend to be more professional than their lower level peers, including post-campaign reporting of results, proper contracts, and timeliness of work. The mid-level influencer level is a great place to discover talented people before they reach celebrity status. At this point, brands will want to establish long-term relationships with influencers, and they

---

8   Myriah Andrson, "What Are Micro-Influencers & Why Are They So Effective?" Impact, February 8, 2019, https://www.impactbnd.com/blog/power-of-micro-influencers.

have the potential to break into a large influencer base that is on an upward spiral. This is also an excellent networking opportunity to gain access to other similar or slightly larger-sized influencers. While all partners should be treated with respect, this is the level in which brands can increase their support by making their influencers feel especially valued and important. Remember, influencers worked hard to get to this level, so they will expect that validation.

Large Influencers (100K–1M followers)

Influencers often experience a plateau in their audience size between the 100,000–1 million mark. On one hand, they won't have to work as hard to maintain constant growth. On the other, this is also the period in which they may start to experience a slight decline in engagement. It is inevitable that as influencers grow, they will begin to lose touch with their relationship to their audience in some capacity. For example, their direct messages from followers will increase drastically, and their inbox will become flooded with brand offers and spam. Because it is much more difficult to keep up with the demands of being a large influencer, some brands and followers will give up and look elsewhere. Conversely, this is also the time in which brand-collaboration requests will double, if not triple. It is critical that influencers stay true to their audience and authenticity during this time. Branching out with collaborations beyond their niche will allow influencers more flexibility in working with those who share their vision. For example, if a brand is not meeting the influencer's worth or is offering a product or service they do not believe in, they won't feel compelled to collaborate with that brand. Preserving their image and authenticity will help to retain their audience, especially their core and most loyal followers.

In many ways, large influencers are mini celebrities. They may be recognized in public and are bombarded with requests at a rate that some might find surprising. Large influencers should be treated much in the same way as celebrities with a large following. Because it's much more difficult to reach influencers at this level for collaboration, unless the brand is already well-known, brands may go through an agent or assistant at this level rather than the influencer directly. So expect a high level of professionalism. It is critical to set clear expectations and have sound contracts in place that protect the brand.

Mega Influencers (1M+)

This is the point at which influencers know they have made it. Collaboration opportunities are abundant. Even if people don't follow the influencer, they are likely a household name. At this point the only thing mega influencers need to do is maintain the status quo and their authenticity. Mega influencers might pursue higher levels of collaborations and demand more compensation. They may even completely evolve their account out of its original niche.

Mega influencers can range from one million to 100 million followers and beyond. As such, working with them will be like working with celebrities. Brands can be made with just a single post, or they could waste enormous sums of money on campaigns that get them nowhere. For the most part, these influencers are out of reach for most brands, except in rare cases where an influencer takes interest in a small company. This is like winning the lottery. It's always worth it for small brands to set their sights high, but it's important to have an alternative strategy or backup plan. Even larger brands might find a much better return by working with smaller influencers.

BRAND SPOTLIGHT

THE MODERN NURSERY

www.plantsbypost.com

Instagram: @_plantsbypost_

About The Modern Nursery

As third-generation greenhouse growers in Northern California, the Modern Nursery is committed to delivering products with principles that have always been at the root of their family owned and operated business—to grow the best selection of plants with quality always striving to be better.

An interview with Andi, Digital Marketing Coordinator

Q: What do you look for in an influencer partnership?

A: There are so many things to look for in an influencer partnership. We focus on an alignment of interest and product—for example, if the influencer knows of us or posts about plants in general; how our products fit into their lifestyle and business; and if our product organically fits into their feed, versus feeling forced. We also prioritize how well we can get along with the influencer. In a world of constant communication and exposure, it's important to us here to associate with kind, thoughtful, and aware individuals.

Q: What are the difficulties of working with influencers?

A: Timely communication is the biggest challenge. Both parties are usually quite busy with their own work, so managing to coordinate time can be difficult. It's always a good idea to start as early as possible when planning a collaboration.

Q: What about the pluses?

A: Gaining exposure to a lot of people that otherwise wouldn't have heard of us is a huge plus. Another plus is that we're given the chance to build a relationship with each influencer. We consider it no different than networking, which helps to ensure that we'll have more opportunities to work with the influencer again in the future.

Q: What are the titles of the people who work with influencers at your company, and are they responsible for other duties?

A: I, Andi, am our digital-marketing coordinator and Sami is in charge of purchasing, as well as supervisor/ general manager of our small team. Both Sami and I have many responsibilities, which is likely the reason Influencer Marketing hasn't been a top priority at the moment.

This complete interview is available in Appendix F on page 231.

SUMMARY

The reality is that very few influencers will become mega-influencers. Those who make it from zero to a million-plus followers are influencers who have stayed true to themselves and to their followers. This is not an easy feat. There will inevitably be bumps along the way, as with growth comes more challenges. The ones who do succeed in this market, however, don't do so through a stroke of luck. With enough hard work, perseverance, and authenticity, almost anyone can reach their goals. Brands need to understand that while influencers may not be who they're used to working with, influencers deserve just as much respect as anyone else. If a brand can collaborate early on with an up and coming influencer, there is potential for a lasting and profitable partnership.

Why Influencer Marketing?

- Influencer Marketing works within any budget
- Influencers have a higher trust with their audience
- Influencer Marketing provides measurable data and metrics
- Influencers can be brand storytellers at a fraction of the cost

There are essentially three kinds of influencers:

1. **Public Figures**
   - Larger accounts that belong to well-known people
   - Hold influence because of who they are outside the digital world
   - Optimal for Influencer Marketing partnerships with large budgets
2. **Makers**
   - Most niche-form of influence, with large impact
   - Following based on something they create that can be purchased
   - Can push a brand that they use and their followers would be interested in using
3. **Content Creators**
   - Most sought-after type of influencer
   - Have influence because of something they have created from nothing

Content creators come in different sizes:

Influencer Type	# of Followers	Distinction
Nano-influencers	0–3K	Just starting out Good choices for affiliate marketing programs Highly engaged and responsive audience
Micro-influencers	3K–20K	Ideal for small- to midsize-company collaborations Decent size audience with a high engagement rate
Mid-level influencers	20K–100K	Collaborating with brands more frequently than micro-influencers More experienced in brand collaborations and have better judgment
Large influencers	100K–1M	Very experienced May have branched out from niche Ideal for brands with large marketing budgets
Mega influencers	1M+	Have absolute control over all collaborations Likely have an agent Expensive price tag

2. BECOMING AN INFLUENCER

WHY BECOME AN INFLUENCER?

The internet has created a golden age for those who wish to become celebrities. One no longer has to hope to be discovered by a large corporation. Instead, we now have a direct line to the public. As long as someone can find a way to resonate with people and grow an audience, they can become an influencer. With the right tools and mindset, anyone can create a loyal following and fan base. But why would anyone want to do this? Maybe they've grown tired of their current career and dream of a life working for themselves. Perhaps they see other people in their age group becoming famous as influencers. Maybe they want to shed light on an issue close to their heart. Maybe some are using influencing as a way to drive more traffic to their own business, or maybe they simply want to make more money and become famous.

Whatever the reason is, that is their *why*. Knowing one's *why* will help them better understand how to market themselves, and if and how brands will approach them. For many, their *why* is money. If it isn't, it will be a nice bonus to one's success. Likewise, an influencer's success directly correlates to their personal branding and standing out in an already oversaturated industry. It's important not to overlook the value in personal branding, because that is what will form a foundation or destroy an influencer's growth. Before starting out, influencers should have a solid business plan for the niche in which they aim to operate (e.g. beauty, lifestyle, skincare, etc.). This will help lay the foundation necessary before branching out into other verticals.

However, very few people who set out to become an influencer actually earn income from their efforts. There are many ways to make a living, and any path that has more sellers than buyers (such is the case with influencers) is going to be a harder road. This is why it's important for influencers' *why* to be more than just getting rich. Influencers will likely spend a lot more money than they earn in return while they are establishing their name. If the primary goal for becoming an influencer is money, the novelty will wear off pretty quickly. It can take a lot of time and effort before an influencer earns a paycheck for what they do, and if their followers sense their lack of authenticity, they will leave them for someone else. Plus, these influencers are likely to quit the market long before cutting a paycheck. If, on the other hand, influencers choose their path because of a genuine passion rather than what they may get in return, then they are more likely to push forward when times get tough to achieve their ultimate goal. It's OK to want to make money through Instagram or YouTube. It's even OK for this to be a primary goal, but making money is a business that requires self-investment, education, growth, and partnering with professionals.

FOR BRANDS

With a creative approach, businesses can use the influence and skills of social-media users to achieve their business or philanthropic goals. Influencer Marketing is a rapidly growing method for reaching a large audience. This form of marketing is not for every business—it will depend on the target audience, budget, brand, and brand aspirations. The products a business sells have a lot to do with whether or not it should pursue Influencer Marketing. Even its goals should be carefully considered. For example, is the intention to sell a product or increase awareness of an issue or brand? Either way, businesses should be looking at Influencer Marketing as an opportunity to get ahead of their competition, if they haven't already been left behind.

The more brands get on board with Influencer Marketing, the more competition there will be. And because social media is changing so rapidly, there are always new opportunities for differentiation and creative profit-making strategies to those who are willing to put in the effort and stay on the cutting edge.

For a brand that executes this well, Influencer Marketing is a method of reaching more people for less money, for saving money on content creation, and for soliciting helpful input from those with a finger on the pulse of the current culture. Working with influencers lets businesses leverage the trust those influencers have built with their audience in ways that were never before possible through traditional celebrity or expert endorsements. The primary difference between traditional marketing and Influencer Marketing is that consumers feel personally connected to influencers, which naturally garners greater trust. Influencers appear more authentic and often only work with brands they would actually use, regardless of a paycheck.

In short, Influencer Marketing can yield a far greater return on investment than many other forms of marketing. Even so, Influencer Marketing is not for every brand. In fact, it's probably not for most. But for those that can make it work, Influencer

Marketing is perhaps the greatest marketing opportunity that has been created since the advent of marketing itself.

FINDING YOUR NICHE

Discovering your niche and the vertical in which you'll operate will be the single most important thing you do on your path to becoming an influencer. A vertical is a group of businesses or non-profits that serve a similar niche. For example: Glossier, Maybelline, and BECCA are in the cosmetics vertical. Within most verticals, the digital space is already over-saturated.[9] To be successful in this virtual world, you *must stand out*. Ask yourself these questions to help determine your niche:

- What am I most passionate about?
- Am I able to share my passion in a constructive and impactful way?
- If I don't have something I'm incredibly passionate about, what is something I would like to learn?
- What are traits about myself that others have commended me for?
- What verticals do I feel are lacking in social representation?
- What content am I most inspired to create?

Finding your niche might not happen overnight, so don't sweat it if you haven't come up with anything just yet. The best thing you can do to move forward will simply be to start. During the grace period of starting and building a following, you can experiment with what you enjoy talking or posting about. This

---

9   Leanne Luce, "How Can Marketers Deal with an Oversaturated Digital Space? Turn Back to Physical Products,"Adweek, August 2, 2018, https://www.adweek.com/brand-marketing/how-can-marketers-deal-with-an-oversaturated-digital-space-turn-back-to-physical-products/.

is the sweet spot where you're not directly tied to one particular vertical or niche. During this time, you should discover not only what is most important to you, but also what your audience responds to best. You should also consider what content you are most inspired to create, as it will be indicative of the platform to which you will dedicate most of your time. To help determine your platform, ask yourself these questions:

- Do I dream of creating beautifully edited videos?
- Am I most passionate about photography or static content?
- Do I love to write?
- Is creating new, information-rich short content what I am best at?

Most influencer success will come with a cohesive marketing strategy across whatever social channels one chooses to engage. However, these questions will help you determine which platform to start with and ultimately dedicate the most effort to. If you love to write, perhaps creating a standard website blog would be in your best interest. If you're passionate about photography, an Instagram account might be the best platform to share your skills.

The key is to choose the channel that will best showcase your skills. That will be the platform through which you dedicate the most time and effort. The most successful content creators are those who have found a sweet spot between their passion and the platform through which to share it.

One common mistake to avoid is trying to do too many things in too many places. If you want to be an influencer on both Instagram and YouTube, understand that your workload will double, making it twice as difficult to stand out from the crowd. The same goes for your focus. Don't try to be everything to everyone. Focus on just one single path until it makes strategic sense to pivot. There is a difference between starting with too many ideas and pivoting to a new idea when what you're doing isn't working. Better yet, your pivots should come when you discover that something is working *better* than what you're already doing.

While a separate website or blog can be important assets, understand that they will create a lot more work for you to maintain. Only create a website when you feel you absolutely need it. You can always create one as you grow—just make sure you've secured the domain names ahead of time. Whenever possible, direct all your energy into a single platform. This will help your audience know exactly where to find you. It will also eliminate a lot of extra work.

As with influencers, brands should be wary of spreading their investment too thin across many different niches and platforms. Unless the brand is well known and experienced, it is better to start with a small niche on a single platform. Once that is successful, companies can look to expand and diversify.

To begin, it's important to examine social-media platforms for similar companies and brands. If there is a gap, then that can mean the product isn't well suited for Influencer Marketing. This can be frustrating for many B2B models or products/services that do not demonstrate well in the social-media format. Products that tend to do very well on Instagram *look* great and are easy to understand. YouTube is a great place for products and services that rely heavily on video content. While video options are available on Instagram, most users have not transitioned to using them on YouTube. It's important to be where your audience is, rather than fight against this trend.

If a product is gaining a lot of exposure on one particular channel, this is a good place to start to explore your own Influencer Marketing campaigns. You may find the existing methods oversaturated. However, utilizing these methods will allow for valuable experience and practice to help navigate the marketplace. Once you're confident in the knowledge and practices, you can begin to employ more creativity to differentiate yourself from the competition.

BRAND SPOTLIGHT

OUTREACH

www.outreach.io

About Outreach.io

Outreach uses up-and-coming individuals to model their software to the public. From social events to conventions and trade shows, influencers are helping drive traffic and sales for business assets. The term influencer hasn't quite reached this market but that isn't holding them back! They are forging the way and helping reform how we think of influence.

An interview with Max Altschuler, vice president of marketing at Outreach

Q: Who is your perfect influencer and how are you reaching them?

A: LinkedIn is like the Instagram of business. As companies change how we reach our customers, we are seeing a shift in how each platform is used. LinkedIn provides a place to teach a potential client as well as build a relationship and foundation that encourages organic sales and growth. With the knowledge of our ideal customer, we can reach out to people as potential influencers. We have dialed in the best size of a person or company to invest our influencer budget in, and where they are in their career. We know we want them to be up-and-coming and provide equal amounts of give and take. Since we know who our ideal influencer is, we can hone in on those metrics as we build relationships.

Q: How are you tracking the worth of you Influencers?

A: The matrix for seeing the worth of our influencer programs is slightly different for business-to-business arrangements. While a traditional influencer arrangement may focus on impressions and sales, Outreach.io focuses on lead generation and people moving through our internal pipeline. Maybe a client who fizzled out is rejuvenated, or maybe there is a net new client who comes out of an event. Our focus is slightly different, but in the end it is still about growth and getting your name out there.

Q: What kind of strategies are you using to protect and ensure growth for your company?

A: We are aware that protecting our company and our 140,000-plus sales professionals is very important. So as we work with influencers, we have some firewalls in place. First, we make sure all contracts have a capped budget increase as well as a non-compete aspect. Second, we plan our influencers by geography of growth and as part of our big-picture marketing plan, each aspect works together with the others. Outreach.io also focuses on both companies so we are prospecting and nurturing our current clients. As a startup we know the importance of growth and how that can change our overall strategy, but we also see this with our influencers. We want to see the people and companies we work with grow, but also know that means that contracts may need to be adjusted, and some influencers may need to be let go so that they can continue their own personal path. That is one of the main reasons our marketing plan is restructured yearly and assessed often.

This complete interview is available in Appendix F on page 234.

PLATFORM SELECTION

A budding influencer faces perhaps no more important decision than which platform they will focus on to build their audience. This section is devoted to helping you understand the platforms and give you tools for how to choose and start building wherever you land. First, let's review a list of the most popular platforms.

Platform	# of Users	Vertical	Primary User Age Range
Facebook	1.6B+ daily	Social Networking	13–65 year olds
Instagram	1B+ monthly	Photo/Video Sharing	18–24 year olds
Twitter	125M+ daily	Microblogging Tweets	18–49 year olds
Tumblr	500M+ monthly	Microblogging	18–29 year olds

LinkedIn	303M+ monthly	Business & Employment	18–50 year olds
WhatsApp	1.5B+ monthly	Messaging	25–29 year olds
Pinterest	291M+ monthly	Image Sharing	< 34 year-old females
YouTube	2B+ monthly	Video Sharing	18–44 year olds
TikTok	500M+ monthly	Media Video Sharing	18–24 year olds
Snapchat	203M+ daily	Multimedia Messaging	13–24 year olds

Now that you've decided what you want to share with the world, the next step is to determine *how* to share it. For example, you may take amazing photographs, but how can you ensure people not only see them, but also actually like them? Social-media growth can be tricky, as users of all platforms are often hit by ever-changing algorithms, competitors, and market saturation.

Personal Branding

Start with the basics. Focus on your personal branding. What will your name, or handle, be? Your name and handle should accurately reflect who you are and the type of content you are engaging. Your name will be the first thing your audience and brands will see. It is critical to remember these points when creating a name:

- You may find that you're not the only one with your chosen name in your desired space. If this is the case, you might want to come up with another name. Alternatively, you may want to consider branding yourself with your actual name. You could also choose a pen name that stands out and follows the principles listed below.

- Keep in mind that if you choose your personal name or a pen name, these words have no meaning to the public other than perhaps associations they already have based on previous experiences. This means you will have to start from scratch when creating space in their mind about who you are and what you stand for. The benefit to this is you can make your personal name mean anything you want. On the other hand, no one will know anything about your brand without gaining further information on your content. Every second counts. The average human attention span is eight seconds.[10] So, if you don't hook your audience within that time frame, they will keep scrolling. Furthermore, using keywords for your SEO (search-engine optimization) content will help your audience find you without ever knowing your name. Appearing in search results on Google, YouTube, or Instagram is critical for growing your following.

- If you're not using your personal name or a pen name, your brand name should reflect your niche. It's how you will be found by both audience members and brands alike that are searching for your niche.

- Your name should be easy to read and understand. You don't want a name that's difficult to pronounce or overly long. It should not include numbers or symbols, aside from dashes or periods.

- If you don't yet have a solid understanding of the niche in which you plan to operate, consider the future possibilities of your account. When it comes to a name, simplicity is golden. Having a name that can seamlessly cross ver-

---

10   Veronika Baranovska, "9 Social Media Trends for 2019 from Social Media Week in London," Sendible, December 13, 2018, https://www.sendible.com/insights/social-media-trends-from-smwldn.

ticals will help you to avoid any necessity to rebrand. For example, if your name is @skincare_lover then you will be incredibly limited to the skincare vertical. This might not be a problem initially, but as you grow in followers, it will limit your possibilities of collaborating with brands outside of the skincare vertical. This will force you to either limit yourself to the skincare vertical or rebrand. Depending on your audience and size, this could drastically affect your engagement.

- Your name should be forever. It is *your* personal brand. It is what your audience will grow to know and trust. It is what brands will look for. It is how your members will refer others to you. It is critical that if you wish to change your name or account handle it should be done at, or prior to, reaching 10,000 followers. This gives your audience time to adjust without your engagement plummeting. It also prevents you from going through a lengthy process of changing your social links on other platforms and delivering notices to current or potential brands. As a marketing best-practice, one should never change branding unless it's a life-or-death situation for the brand. You may be tempted by assuming that your following will adjust, but it could very well mean starting from scratch again. Ensure your name fits within this criterion, or at least make the change now, before reaching the 10,000-follower mark.

Once you've decided on a name, act fast. Regardless of the primary platform you choose, it's a good practice to create all social media accounts with the same handle. Even if you don't plan to utilize all of them, securing your handle is important so that no one else uses and capitalizes on your name. It is equally as important that if you decide to branch out into other channels down the road, your name is already secured. You will want to claim your handle in as many places as possible, even when new platforms emerge.

Instagram is an ideal place to start. Instagram is one of the most engaged-in and utilized social channels of this decade, with over one billion users.[11] Even if you plan to post primarily on other channels, Instagram is the ideal tool to cross-promote your content. You want to drive as much traffic as possible back to your primary platform, and this is often achieved by cross-channel promotion.

Domains

You will also want to secure a *.com* name, even if you plan to use another extension for shorter length. Many consumers still don't understand other extensions such as .biz or .name. Many people tend to consider anything other than a *.com* or *.org* to be less reliable or trustworthy. It's OK to use a new extension, especially since it increases the options for your name. Still, you should try to get the *.com* and forward it to the domain you end up using. If you don't plan to have a website, that's OK too. Just forward the domains to the main page that you are using. For example, if your brand name is Romantic Pencils, you will want to get @romanticpencils on Instagram, Facebook, YouTube, etc. You will also want to get www.romanticpencils.com. If that's not available, get www.romanticpencils.whatever and then also get www.romanticpencils.whatever.com and forward it to the main domain. Or, just forward both to @romanticpencils on Insta-

---

11   Jenn Chen, "Important Instagram Stats You Need to Know for 2020," Sprout Social, https://sproutsocial.com/insights/instagram-stats/.

gram, YouTube, or whichever platform you end up using as your primary account.

Blogging

After securing your social channels comes the more laborious task of setting up your blog. Every content creator should have a blog. If you're aspiring to be a blogger, a website will be your primary source of truth. However, even if you don't plan on blogging, it is still something important to consider. A blog is an incredibly important source because it will likely be the place brands will search for potential collaboration. It's a place where you can showcase your portfolio or your work, a place through which you can be contacted, and a platform that you can utilize to cross promote to other platforms. A personal webpage will also allow you to optimize your ranking in Google search results, which will become critical for your personal-brand awareness down the road.[12] You will want to dominate the first page of Google (remember—eight seconds) and ensure that anything negative or embarrassing is not there. When you garner a large enough audience, you will likely be Googled. For example, brands will Google you for potential collaboration. Your audience will Google you to share your content with others, and potential followers will Google you to see what you're all about. Either way, the more often you show up in Google search results, the better your account will perform.

When creating a personal blog or webpage, you should try to think as far into the future as possible to ensure you are setting it up correctly the first time around. This will prevent you from having to spend extra time, money, and developer re-

---

12   Neil Patel, "Personal SEO: 14-Point Checklist to Dominate Your Personal Brand on Google," Neilpatel.com, https://neilpatel.com/blog/personal-branding-seo/.

sources down the road. This means ensuring that the website provider services are enough to cover large amounts of traffic, constant content, design, and back-end engineering changes. When setting up a personal blog it's easy to fall into the trap of a hosted service such as Wix or Medium. While both are easy and quick solutions, hosted web platforms such as these are not designed to accommodate large amounts of traffic. They're difficult to manage and customize from an engineering standpoint, and they are more challenging to work with when integrating third-party tools such as Google Analytics, Google Ad words, etc. Hosted website platforms also make it incredibly difficult, if not impossible, to migrate content in the event that you want to change platforms. To make matters worse, since you're not responsible for hosting, you might find buried in the fine print that they own all content uploaded using their servers.

Tools

To quickly and easily set up a self-hosted website (meaning that you pay an independent party to host your website online), you should utilize tools such as:

- Wordpress.org—A platform that allows for any type of customization. Be careful to not confuse this for wordpress. com, which is a host, similar to Bluehost below. While you can use WordPress for hosting with a small monthly fee, you can also download the WordPress system for free and use it on any other host you wish to use. The free WordPress is at the *.org* location.

- Bluehost—A third party website-hosting provider, which allows for hosting changes related to traffic volume and other factors.

- ThemeForest—A bountiful and inexpensive source for WordPress themes that you can install and modify yourself with zero to very little knowledge of programming.

- iStock photo—A great source for video, illustrations, and images without resorting to stealing content from the internet (something ethical content creators never do).

- Domains.google.com—a low-cost and easy-to-use domain registry service. Besides low-cost registry fees, you can use Google to establish free privacy, which means the public won't know the true owner of the domain. The domain you register on Google must be pointed at whatever host you select for the website to work properly. Tutorials and help documents on both your host and domain registrar can help you to accomplish this.

- Upwork.com—A marketplace of freelancers who can help you with just about anything, from setting up your website to assisting you virtually. Prices per hour range from as little as four dollars to over one hundred dollars. You can find contractors around the world who fit your needs and expectations.

- Fiverr.com—A freelancer marketplace much like Upwork, but on a lower scale. Freelancers on Fiverr sell five-dollar gigs, but don't let the price fool you. Most projects will likely cost much more than five dollars. However, if you're looking for something quick and easy, Fiverr may be your best bet.

While these tools may seem daunting at first, they are not difficult to navigate or set up. Knowing which tools to use will save you time and money in the long run. Utilizing these tools will also allow for faster and easier email configurations as well as smoother integrations with other tools such as analytics, mail subscriptions, and email-subscription lists. These features may not be top of mind when setting up your webpage, but as you grow they will become crucial for both your personal-brand growth and how you appear to potential companies looking for collaboration. Brands will often examine your traffic engagement across multiple platforms when determining if you'd be a good fit. For example, you may only have 20,000 Instagram followers, but analytics on your blog could show 100,000 monthly viewers. You would only gain insight into this data by having an analytics platform initiated on your webpage. Being able to provide this data to potential brands is often the difference between those who acquire brand collaborations and those who do not.

Outsourcing

If you are intimidated by setting any of this up, or if you just don't have the time, you can always hire other people and services to do it for you. Some platforms simply make it all easier for you, such as www.squarespace.com, or you can use a freelancer community to post a job and hire an expert. You should be able to hire someone through Upwork to do all the work for you for between one hundred dollars and $1,000, depending on what you want. Be wary of services that charge too much for all of this. If you don't know where to start, enlist the help of someone who does this frequently.

If you are using a service like WordPress, you can download themes through sites like ThemeForest for between thirty and sixty dollars. Within reason, these themes are also customizable. Depending on your budget, you have unlimited control with WordPress. With Squarespace, you are limited in your control but the process is much simpler and cheaper in many cases than building something from scratch.

INFLUENCER SPOTLIGHT

MORGAN HALEY

Instagram: @FindingMorganTyler, previously @the_southern_yogi

Morgan Haley is an influential figure in the health and wellness space, specializing in her yoga practice, where she reaches an Instagram audience of nearly 500,000 followers. She's been through the ups and downs of what it means to be a social-media influencer and a small-business owner.

Q: Did you ever set out to become an influencer?

A: You know, I never, ever in a million years thought I'd be a social-media 'influencer.' When I first hopped on IG, it was just for fun—like everyone else. I was working in my field as a vascular sonographer and then switched over to being a barista so I could focus more on yoga. Once I started posting snippets of my yoga journey, my account blew up. Like, went from two hundred followers to 100,000 in under a year. That's when brands started reaching out to me, people wanting to pay me for posts. I was both flattered and shocked. This began my journey of making Instagram my full-time job. It kind of fell straight into my lap.

Q: Have you ever experienced any of the negative side-effects of social media?

A: Oh, absolutely. Every choice you make is scrutinized by thousands of people. It's a bit crippling at times. I've had death threats made, hate-mail sent, and even people spying on me at local restaurants and gyms only to report my every move to troll accounts. It used to make me want to never post again. But over the years I've learned you can only feel sad for those people, and the lives they must lead have led them to target so much hate towards someone they don't even know.

Q: What piece of advice would you give to brands?

A: Stop sending mass emails out. We know when you've sent the same email to hundreds of other influencers. It definitely doesn't make us feel special or that you 'really loved our page.' Personal emails and attention to details go a long way.

Q: Do you have an example of a collaboration with a brand that went poorly?

A: I collaborated with a major mall clothing store once for an activewear campaign. Somewhere along the way there was a miscommunication, and weeks after I'd posted this campaign for them, they noticed I hadn't added one specific word to my caption. They wanted me to redo the entire campaign. I felt a bit taken advantage of, as it wasn't noticed immediately, and the ads had been up on my page for a while, giving them massive amounts of exposure. Now they wanted me to do it all again. I refused, and then they refused to send the winners of my giveaway posts their gift cards. So not only did I not get paid for that campaign, but I had to purchase the gift cards myself and mail them out.

Q: What are your thoughts on how influencing impacts daily life?

A: I think it's only negatively increased the comparison game, and comparison is the thief of joy. People are looking at others' homes, relationships, bodies, and just lifestyles in general and wondering if they could do better. No one waters their own grass anymore, and everyone yearns for their neighbor's instead. The grass is greener where you water it! On the flip side—I think it's allowed so many people our age to completely thrive with entrepreneurship and small businesses. It's created a community where you aren't simply limited to a brick and mortar clientele, but can offer your passions and business to people globally with the click of a button.

Q: What is your least favorite part of working with brands?

A: I'd say the rules. Ha-ha. I hate complying with contractual obligations. Every brand or company has something they want you to do or say—whether it's specific wording or verbiage, or how a photo looks that isn't quite 100 percent authentic to you and your page.

Q: Is blogging your full-time job?

A: I'm not so much a blogger (in the writing sense) as an instructor and lifestyle influencer. I make my living selling my yoga videos on a subscription-based app, and also selling my personal merchandise like face masks, scrunchies, headbands and ball caps on my website. But yes—Instagram, and all it entails, is my full-time gig!

This complete interview is available in Appendix E on page 218.

Investing Across Platforms

In most cases, businesses have more resources than individual influencers, so it's more appropriate for a brand to maintain many different platform channels. However, just like influencers, brands should not try to be everything to everyone. Organizations should make the best use of channels and platforms that resonate most with their consumers and best fit their products, services, and appeal.

A brand's considerations on platform selection are different from those of an individual influencer. For example, a brand is most concerned with reaching a wider audience that spans across several platforms. Where an influencer is likely to want to focus on one or two platforms that most resonate with their following, a brand wants to reach consumers who may be highly engaged across several channels. For the purpose of maximizing return through Influencer Marketing, it's important for a brand to have a strong presence on the same network as their brand ambassador. This is so consumers can find consistent content that resonates with what they expect of their chosen influencer and platform. For example, a brand with poor or little Instagram presence is going to receive a much lower return on an Instagram-based influencer campaign than another brand that invests heavily in this platform. Consumers on each network have different expectations for engagement, post frequency, content, look, feel, and tone. They may love an influencer and their posts about a brand, but when they click through to check out the brand or place an order, they may be turned off to find a brand that doesn't seem relevant.

Even the same consumers operate and have different expectations as they move through social networks. If consumers viewed their various social networks in the same way, they wouldn't have a need for more than one. One person may go to

Pinterest for remodeling inspiration and be turned off to find self-promotional content about an upcoming album release. However, if they encountered this same material on Facebook from a musician page they follow, they might share it with several friends who like the same music. Plus, users can become annoyed by multiple posts on the same day on Instagram but expect or even enjoy it on Twitter.

In short, brands should be more platform fluid than influencers. They need to be where their consumers are. As such, they should align their social-media investment with the same platforms as the influencers with whom they want to work, the same platforms as their consumers are most likely to be operating within. As they invest in these platforms, they should focus on working with people who understand those platforms and the nuances that make each of them unique. Brands must strike a balance between authenticity to the platform, authenticity with the influencers they sponsor, and authenticity to their market position. Those who accomplish this well can see a remarkably efficient return on their advertising spend when compared to other forms of market exposure.

WHEN CAN YOU EXPECT TO START MAKING MONEY?

Earning money on social media is a lot like earning money from being a professional musician, painter, or author. A lot more people want to do it than there are opportunities for well-paid roles. Even those who are very talented at what they do will not likely earn a living from their efforts. Whether or not someone makes it largely has to do with luck, being in the right place at the right time, and good marketing. This isn't to say it's impossible. New influencers emerge every day, and some will go on to earn a living from their work. This can happen right away for some, but others may work for years before they legitimately make a living from it and consider themselves full-time.

This can cause some confusion because people have different definitions of what it means to be a full-time blogger. For example, many people who claim to be full-time influencers earn their money in other ways or don't require an income. It's easy to be a full-time blogger when you don't need to make money. Others can grow much more quickly than an average influencer. This could be because they have a large budget for advertising. Or, they have the flexibility and free money to hire the best talent, own the best gear, and travel to the most beautiful locations.

Due to all these factors, it's important to not compare yourself to others in these situations. In fact, if you want to be an influencer, it's better to go into it without any expectation of earning an income. There may be a few years, if not more, before you can expect a return on your investment of time and money. If you expect to earn an income from Influencer Marketing within a given time frame and you don't reach that goal, you may find yourself losing interest and giving up. But if you start out to have fun, express yourself, or share on social media for personal reasons, then you won't be disappointed if you don't earn an income. Removing this burden is an important way to reveal your authenticity to your audience. You also won't be tempted to take brand deals that don't align with your values just for a paycheck.

On the other hand, earning an income from social media is not impossible. Anyone can build a following over time and turn that following into cash or free products. If you follow best practices, keep learning, and stick with it, you can certainly expect to achieve your goals. The question is, how much are you willing to learn and grow as you go? And will you give up before you get there?

Brands should try to understand the motivations and hopes of the influencers with whom they work. Chances are, even if you are a small company, you likely have more flexibility within your budget than the influencer does. For small influencers, even a small payment can go a long way towards building a strong and lasting relationship. Hire good people who get the results you want and with whom you enjoy working. Then pay them as much as you can afford. If they're good at what they do, they are likely working diligently to share their talents, time, and equipment to help you grow and profit. Remember that just because you can find influencers who will do the same amount of work for less doesn't mean you should.

INFLUENCER SPOTLIGHT

BRENDA STEARNS

Content creator
Instagram: @she_plusfive

Q: Do you want to be an influencer?

A: I believe we all are influencers in our own way. We all have a circle of people whom we can influence for good or bad. In the world of social media, I have been given the opportunity and honor to have a big audience. While that was never my initial goal, I guess in that sense, yes, I am an influencer.

Q: If Instagram/YouTube were to be permanently deleted, what would you do?

A: Go on with my life and move onto the next thing that God brings my way. I truly believe there are seasons in life for everything, and change can be a good thing.

Q: Have you ever experienced the negative side-effects of social media (bullying, trolls, etc.)? How has this affected you?

A: Yes, daily. In the beginning of my social-media journey, it would affect me a lot. I would focus on that negative comment, unconsciously letting it affect how I went on about the rest of the day. I think now things have changed a bit; I've grown some thick skin. Comments don't hurt as much. Eighty percent of the time, people genuinely care and think they're giving good advice by telling you how to live your life, etc. There's always that 20 percent who are plain just trying to poke at you. Just smile and move on. It's not worth our time or energy.

Q: How is this influencer movement negatively or positively affecting society?

A: What should influencers do to be a more positive influence? Influencers need to be more genuine about their collaborations. Taking into consideration your audience and their loyalty to your platform. Not just doing it for the money.

This complete interview is available in Appendix E on page 199.

SUMMARY

While becoming an influencer is an exciting prospect, it's not as easy as it may look. Followers only see one side of the coin—someone who is popular, engaging, and making money from doing something they love. Behind the scenes there are countless things to consider. From choosing a long-lasting handle, niche, and platform, to setting up a website, securing the same handle across various channels, and navigating SEO content.

The platform you end up utilizing will be dependent on the type of content you hope to generate. However, you should always secure all social handles when starting out. This will ensure your handle is available in the future if you wish to branch out and prevent anyone else from impersonating you.

At first, you might not know what type of content you hope to create in the long term. In this case, Instagram is a good starting point, as it is one of the most utilized social channels by brands, influencers, and consumers alike.

After establishing a social account, you should also secure a domain and blog. Even if you do not plan to be a blogger, having a website will allow people to find you online, independent of a platform. It will give them the opportunity to understand what you are about and how to get in contact with you.

It's important for brands to recognize the effort it takes for influencers to get to where they are and have that reflected in what they're willing to give in return. While it may take time before you start seeing a paycheck, it is possible to make a living doing what you love. As long as you put in the time and energy and are able to deliver what your followers want, anything is possible.

First steps to becoming an influencer:

Find your niche:

- What are you passionate about? (e.g. nails, environment)
- What are you good at? (e.g. photography, writing)
- What do you enjoy? (e.g. public speaking, making collages)

- How can you stand out? (e.g. bold personality, interesting delivery)

Choose your platform:

- Do you like taking photographs? (Instagram)
- Are you engaging/entertaining? (YouTube)
- Can you captivate an audience with writing? (Website)

Brand yourself:

- Choose a unique name that describes your niche.
- Choose a name that's easy to read and understand.
- Brand your name on all platforms.
- Choose a domain for your name.

3. GROWTH

Now that you have the fundamentals (name, associated platforms, and content), how can you optimize your platform(s) to gain attraction, grow your audience, and optimize your brand relationships? Fostering a strong relationship with your audience is the single most important factor in growing a healthy and engaged following.

Brands that work with influencers need to have their own social channels if they're going to get the most out of Influencer Marketing. Just like with influencers, the number of engaged followers you have is critically important to your return on investment. This section will review best practices for building your own social channels, so when customers find your product through your influencer campaigns, they will engage with your brand in a way that fits with your goals.

AUTHENTICITY

FOR INFLUENCERS

As an influencer, honesty and authenticity will determine your success. Your audience expects these traits and is perceptive enough to know when something is contrived. As influencers grow within their vertical, they may become well known by the other accounts operating in the same space. Those who have come before will likely have already been exposed to brands, products, and spaces of contribution. They may have a larger following than newer influencers, causing audiences to overlap. Providing fake content, false reviews, or any other type of malicious content will eventually result in an audience's distrust of their influencer. This will inevitably lead to a decrease in engagement and growth. Untrustworthy influencers will quickly get a bad reputation. Brands see this, resulting in fewer collaborations. Not everything you create has to be perfect. Not every review or content exposure will work out, and negative engagement can result in scathing content or reviews. Just make sure you continue to be transparent with your audience. This way, they will maintain their respect for you. You may lose brands along the way, but know that your audience comes first.

FOR BRANDS

Authenticity is more difficult and complicated for a brand than it is for an individual. A company is made up of lots of people, so it can't be true to itself in the same way that one person can. Individuals are advised to make decisions independent of outside pressures, whereas a brand must often incorporate the ideas of many people into its social-media content. People will come and go from companies, but the brand's authenticity must remain consistent. An influencer can simply ask themselves if they truly want to do something, or if they like one approach over another, whereas a brand must be confident in what it is as a collection of people and ideas before it can fully achieve authenticity. This is why it's so important for a brand to understand and be confident in what it stands for.

A brand should post content and engage with its followers in a way that is consistent with its values and market perception. A good indicator of authenticity for a brand is how it has defined its persona. It's important to invest the time and effort into developing a brand's persona and collective goals. That way your audience will be able to clearly understand your values through your social-media posts and engagement.

CONSISTENCY

An often-overlooked factor of being an influencer, content creator, or personal brand is cohesiveness amongst platforms. Influencers should aim to be easily found, recognizable, and consistent. This is achieved through:

- Maintaining the same name or handle across platforms.
- Ensuring your profile picture is consistent across platforms.
- Using the same hero or banner images where applicable—these are the larger images that appear at the top of many platforms' home pages such as Twitter, Facebook, and LinkedIn.
- Maintaining branding and content cohesiveness—your logo, color palette, and content-editing styles should be the same regardless of the platform they belong to. Your goal is to eventually have content that is recognizable without having your name attached to it.
- Monitoring your posting frequency—this will vary based on your own brand interpretation of platform norms and may not require the same kind of consistency. For example, Twitter is a platform where posting many times in the same day is more acceptable than it is on Instagram, where frequent posting can feel like spam to your users.

While consistency is important for influencers who want to build their audience, brands don't necessarily need to be as concerned with consistency regarding their influencers. If a brand seeks to partner with influencers who match their aesthetic, this is a different consideration. Most brands should be primarily focused on the connection an influencer has with their audience, rather than aesthetic factors. You may be able to find a better deal working with influencers who have managed to create a powerful connection with their audience regardless of how well they follow the rules. This can be a sign that they are so good at connecting with their audience they don't need to follow the same rules as other influencers. Or it could mean they simply don't know what they're doing, which may mean they will work for a better rate than others. In either case, don't be afraid to consider influencers who don't seem to fit the mold of what lies within best practices. Instead, focus on your business objectives and determine if a particular influencer will be the best person to help you achieve your goals.

NICHE

Be yourself. Be unique. Stand out. In the already oversaturated industry of digital influencers there will be many people, just like you, doing the same things as you. They will be photographing the same things, reviewing the same products, and collaborating with the same brands. A simple Google or Instagram search of your favorite product will likely yield a large bucket of the same content, whether it's similarly styled photographs or videos, or the same excited reviews. Eventually it becomes static and boring, and if your audience has already seen the same photo or review a handful of times they will be less likely to engage with yours. Finding your niche *within* your niche is most important. Think back to the earlier question: *What are traits about myself that others have recommended me for?* Utilize these traits about yourself as inputs into the content you create. Perhaps you are well known for your sense of humor. Incorporating this into the content you create will help to set yourself apart.

Similar to individual influencers, brands should seek to establish their own unique niche in their social-media space of choice. Spend the necessary time to monitor your competition or any others that are in your space. Make sure your content and approach to social media is distinctive from your competitors so that you have a strong chance of standing out to consumers. Given the limitless options social-media users have today, there must be a unique and compelling reason for people to follow you, otherwise they'll move on to someone else.

AUDIENCE GROWTH SOURCES

Whether you're an individual breaking into social media for the first time or a brand that has been investing in social media for years, you should keep abreast of the most current and effective strategies for growing your following of engaged fans. The key to growth is maintaining high engagement from your followers. This is done through continuing to remain authentic, thereby increasing your legitimacy with your audience even as you grow. If you don't purchase fake followers (as discussed in the next section), this is a lot easier to say than to do. Social media algorithms tend to show the content of smaller pages to those who follow them. So as you grow, the percentage of people seeing your posts is likely to diminish over time. The opportunities for engaging your followers only lessen as you grow. To maintain the same levels of engagement will require even more compelling content as you increase the size of your audience.

This section reviews a few of the most common methods used for growing your social-media following. Some are more effective than others, while a few options should be avoided altogether. We will review the pros and cons of advertising, collaborations, public relations, cross-promotions, and running your own content.

Advertising

Do not buy followers or engagement. While most platforms are now honing in on this tactic, it's still important to mention. As you start out, you will likely be approached by account-management platforms or services. This is an easy trap to fall into for new influencers, since they may not be privy to these malicious tactics until damage has already been done. Influencers might also be tempted to buy followers in an attempt to cut corners to grow quickly, increasing their chances of working with brands. This will be directly reflected in your account data or statistics. There are a multitude of platforms that provide insights into overall account health. These statistics allow brands, or anyone who's interested, to view your following and engagement statistics. That includes potential bot followers (fake accounts), as there is a correlation between the number of followers and engagement on posted content. For example, if you bought 10,000 followers, but your engagement remained the same as when you had 2,000 followers, then this would be a red flag to both brands and your audience. This fosters ultimate distrust and discredit of an influencer's account. This will hurt influencers in the long run, as brands will not want to work with them, and people will not want to follow someone who appears fake.

Advertising your posts to gain followers is different than buying followers, and it can be a good strategy for growth in some circumstances. In this case, you are paying to put your posts in front of real people who have the choice to engage with your post or follow you. This is the key difference between purchasing followers, which tend to be bots that don't engage, and advertising to gain followers. However, some of the same rules and risks apply as with buying followers. You will want to make sure the audience you are gaining through advertising is actually engaging with your posts at an equal or similar rate to your other followers. If you are hoping to gain followers and increase your value to brands, you will also want to make sure the followers you target through advertising are within the target demographics of the brands you want to reach. For example, if you are targeting brands such as Forever 21, you will want to make sure your audience is young, middle class, and in geographic locations where Forever 21 operates.

Advertising to get followers, while not unethical, can be a waste of money and may not help you achieve your goals. Social platforms are built on advertising dollars, but when influencers use this strategy to gain followers, they are competing against much more sophisticated advertising machines. The cost to acquire followers in this way may outpace what you can achieve in return from brand collaborations. Finally, you may find that you have spent a large sum of money to build a following, only to have that following taken away by the platforms that enticed you to advertise to them in the first place. Changing algorithms can prioritize smaller users. So as you grow, platforms may stop showing posts from most influencers in place of posts from friends and families. This is a risky strategy that you should only engage in if you can afford to lose the money you are spending.

Organizations may consider increasing exposure to their target market through advertising, but this can be ineffective if you're not careful. Social platforms want to make it easy for you. They know it feels rewarding for companies to spend to gain followers, because this is a lucrative source of revenue. It's also a way to get brands to spend even more money to have their content shown to those who have followed their pages. But this isn't always the best use of your dollar. Instead of paying money just to gain followers, brands can tangibly see growth through other forms of advertising, since all ads are tied to a page. When viewing your ad, consumers have the chance to click through to your page and follow you. This is a free side-benefit of running ads for another campaign, ideally one that has a clear positive return for every dollar spent.

If you're going to use advertising to gain followers, don't lose sight of your return on investment. Try to project how you will turn those advertising dollars into profit in the form of sales or impact toward your final goal. Too many companies set a goal of adding followers without a clear plan for profiting from that increased followership. These companies often feel like they have to demonstrate their followership growth for credibility, but keep in mind that engagement rates may suffer with the wrong execution of an advertising plan. This could negatively affect your credibility, because those who happen upon your page will see that your followers don't seem to care about your content.

Most platforms today make it very easy to advertise, but it might be worth hiring a freelancer or agency to do this work for you. This cost could be offset in part or entirely on more effective and efficient advertising campaigns that help to move you toward your goal. Freelancers are a good choice for companies who have a social-advertising budget of less than $100,000 per year. Those with higher budgets may want to consider working with an agency instead. Agencies are more expensive, but also more reliable and capable of working effectively with larger budgets.

In any case, be sure to test your campaigns for return. Start small and increase your spending as you improve your return. As you gain confidence that your strategies are working, it's nothing to increase your daily ad spend.

Other Advertising Considerations

Brand growth relies on an effective and cohesive marketing strategy. Your advertisements need to be regular and consistent. Building a recognizable brand image will ultimately lead to higher brand awareness. From a brand perspective, it is critical to identify your marketing goals prior to running advertisements. Defining your key performance indicators (KPIs) will allow you to determine not only the best platform to run advertisements, but the best secondary platforms to boost your holistic campaign effectiveness. For example, imagine you are a health-food brand. You have determined that your campaign goals are brand awareness and subscriptions to your online newsletter. You have 50,000 engaged Instagram followers, but growth is not steady, and you lack conversions to your website.

One campaign advertisement that might be effective would be to run a short Instagram paid advertisement with a call-to-action button, like "learn more," in the post. Couple that with an incentive for new subscribers (such as 10 percent off first order). You also might find it beneficial to place ad spend behind SEO to boost your campaign and let other traffic sources know of the incentive. Advertisements can be more than just an ad spend, SEO, or paid posts. They can utilize influencers who already have engaged audiences to promote your products or services. These can be short campaigns over Facebook stories or Pinterest ads. They could even be something like a contest that requires users to post (essentially boost) a specific piece of content across their channel(s).

BRAND SPOTLIGHT:

PYNE & SMITH CLOTHIERS

www.pyneandsmith.com

Instagram: @pyneandsmithclothiers

An interview with owner Joanna McCartney

Q: What do you look for in an influencer partnership?

A: Good photography, authentic messages, engaged followers, and ethics.

Q: How do you vet influencers to ensure success?

A: I review their social media posts and comments, look at their style and photography, and go from there to see if they are the right fit for our brand.

Q: What characteristics of influencers do you look for (size, brand, demographics, style, etc.)?

A: Usually engagement with their followers takes priority. I usually try to work with influencers that have at least 10,000 followers, but if they have a good message, high engagement with their audience, or really great photos, then I will also consider working with them.

Q: Can you share an example of a negative experience with a campaign?

A: I am pretty picky with influencers, so I haven't had many unsuccessful or bad experiences. But I did work with one influencer (two years ago) who I realized had bought her followers and didn't really seem genuine or care about the product. It taught me to really review their posts and who they work with before I commit to working with influencers.

Q: What social channels do you prefer and why?

A: Instagram and Pinterest. I find that strong imagery can help sell out dresses, so I work on these two platforms as much as possible.

This complete interview is available in Appendix F on page 236.

Contests

Opportunities for growth are plentiful if you know where to look and if you're willing to put in the work. Contests are a win-win for both influencers and brands. They give both sides a chance to reach their intended target audience. When aligning with a brand that knows your following, you can grow in numbers, popularity, and worth, usually with minimal financial risk. There are important action items that can save you time and energy, if you think ahead. Ensure that your expectations are voiced and that you listen to what the brand is looking for as well. Also make sure that what you are asking from your followers is simple.

In these cases it's important to be realistic in your expectations. For example, if you have 105,000 followers and the brand has 75,000, don't expect them to bring more followers to the table. Instead, focus on product or monetary growth. Each contest you perform should provide value to your following, like discovering new products, brands, or influencers. In turn, they will follow through with your ask, whether it be following a brand, signing up for a newsletter, or making a purchase.

When brands align with an influencer for a contest, they not only gain direct access to the influencer's following, but also a potentially new audience. Instead of advertising outside of your demographic, you can gain access to those who fulfill your ideal consumer profile. With a contest, you can open the flood gates directly into your customers' feed, getting your product/brand directly into the hands of more followers. At the same time, you get to reach people who would potentially become new customers. When running contests through influencers, be sure to be direct in your expectations, number of posts, number of photos, length of time, follow-through, and opportunities for follow-up engagement or posts. Always remember to follow up with those who enter the contest. As long as you engage with them, market to them, and follow through with them, you can gain lifelong customers.

Collaborations

Who are you wearing? That is the number-one most asked question on any red carpet. It is also the perfect example of a collaboration where an influencer can fully represent a brand. Making money as an influencer can be a long and rocky road, but collaborating with brands and getting free swag is not nearly as difficult. Using the media kit that will be discussed further in chapter 7 can help you get started. If you know your following and your ideal brand alignment, you can use that data to create new collaborations. It is important for you to also know what the brand's expectations are. Make sure that you are building long-lasting, mutually beneficial relationships. If you don't follow through with the brand's expectations, you may find it hard to keep doing so, not only with them but with other brands as well. Word travels fast if you are not an easy person to work with. In the same respect, word travels *really* fast if you have good follow-through and provide what you promise.

Imagine if the answer to the question "Who are you wearing?" was **your** brand. That is collaboration, a way to get your brand out in the real world and into the hands of your customers. Once again, when joining with an influencer make sure you have made your expectations very clear. A typical collaboration consists of the influencer being provided an item or service in return for sharing their experience and lifestyle with their following. This is a natural format for your potential customers to see who is using your brand. More information on collaborations can be found in chapter 7.

Cross-Promotions

Cross-promoting with other influencers who share some of the same audience demographics can be a great way to quickly increase your following. Like everything else influencer-related, this also needs to be authentic and achieved through a genuine relationship between influencers. Your audience will know otherwise, and you will chance losing credibility. Find ways to promote other accounts without appearing too pushy or obviously promotional. Make it appear natural. For example, two influencers could create a video together and promote it on both of their channels. Each influencer could build up their co-creator and suggest fans follow them if they're interested in a particular form of content. This type of cross-promotion is a real strength for the collaborator. You could even guest-post on each other's blogs, or post a photo of you together doing something authentic on both your accounts and tag each other. You won't likely see a big surge in followers from just one cross-promotion, but if you consistently network and promote other bloggers who share the same audience, over time, you could see results that can easily outperform other tactics for growth. The best part is these followers tend to be highly engaged, since they learned about you from someone they already trust.

A company looking to cross-promote should, for the most part, follow the same guidelines as an individual influencer. The only difference is that brand pages are less personality-centric, so it's not as likely to provide the same kinds of opportunities for cross-promotion. On the other hand, unique opportunities are available for brand cross-promotions. For example, a brand can post content from several individuals, since a brand is made up of many people anyway. This is expected by the followers of a brand. Find an influencer or complimentary brand and share content about them on your page. Ask them to do the same for you in return. Consider using trackable links wherever possible to measure the effectiveness of the cross-promotion. Alternatively, measure your follower count directly before the cross-promotion is launched to identify how many followers resulted from the campaign.

SUMMARY

As an influencer, the key to growing your audience is to remain honest and authentic in all that you do. That way, you can maintain high engagement from your followers, thereby growing your audience. Remember, the key is to make it easy to be found and recognizable. You can do this through maintaining the same name, handle, profile picture, logo, color palette, and banner images across platforms so that your content is easily recognizable. Your posting frequency, however, will depend on the norms of your chosen platform.

There are several ways to grow your audience, but whatever you do, don't buy followers or engagement as it will negatively reflect in your account health. Advertising, on the other hand, can be a good strategy for growth. Contests, collaborations, and cross-promotion can also help to grow your following.

As far as brands are concerned, it's important to establish your own unique niche and develop an effective and cohesive marketing strategy. If you choose to use advertising to gain followers, don't lose sight of your return on investment. Hiring a freelancer or agency to do your advertising work for you is an excellent option for your bottom line.

HOW TO MAKE IT EASY FOR FOLLOWERS TO FIND YOU:

- Have the same name/handle across all platforms.
- Make sure your profile picture is the same across all platforms.
- Use the same hero or banner images across applicable platforms.
- Use the same logo, color palette and style across all platforms.
- Be consistent with your posts, keeping in mind the platform's norms.

DOS AND DON'TS OF INFLUENCING

Do	Don't
Be authentic, yourself	Be fake—your followers will see through you
Gain followers through posts/referrals	Buy followers
Promote brands you believe in	Sell out just for a check
Be professional with collaborations	Use brands for free stuff
Cross-promote with other influencers	Trash talk your competition

4. EVALUATING THE PERFORMANCE OF YOUR SOCIAL PRESENCE

AFTER YOU HAVE SOLID CONTENT UNDER YOUR BELT AND YOU begin to grow, you will be able to unlock the power of data. Using this data to recognize trends will help you to begin growing your account. Once you've reached nano-influencer status (3–10,000 followers), you should be on the lookout for trends in your content that will allow you to optimize your account for maximum growth. While available insights for platforms may differ, you should be able to access and optimize these metrics, such as engagement rate, time-of-day metrics, audience demographics, and referring traffic.

If you're a brand, you should always verify an influencer's following and engagement prior to setting pricing for working with them. Never assume that a large number of followers will result in engagement for your campaign. A number of tools are available for verifying engagement and quantity of bots following someone. Ultimately, you want to verify that this influencer can help you achieve whatever goal you have for the campaign. If that means selling product, you should not only look at their engagement, but also ask to see actual results from past campaigns that are similar to what you want to conduct. Don't be fooled by flashy personalities who show well but don't get results. In the end, it doesn't matter where their followers came from or how long it took them to grow. All that matters is whether or not this influencer can return your investment at a rate better than you can achieve elsewhere. Ignore all other distractions and metrics.

METRICS

Post engagement relates to how many viewers, likes, and comments you receive for a single piece of content, in relation to the number of followers you have. Post engagement will depend on a multitude of factors (some discussed below). To ensure you're posting the right content, it's important to ask yourself, "Is this content valuable?" That may relate to aesthetics (i.e. is my content pleasing to look at?). Or, this could relate to value provided. Sometimes aesthetics alone will be enough to generate decent engagement on a piece of content. More often, depending on your niche, your accompanying post or content caption will be where your audience finds value. If you are not providing valuable content, your engagement will likely reflect that. With the goal of account growth in mind, you should be working toward creating a consistent content schedule. This schedule will be determined by the types of content that have proven to be best performing. To determine the health or engagement of your content, pull a weekly or monthly content report to determine which pieces of content are performing the best. Four important metrics to consider are:

- Follower-count to engagement-ratio
- Time-of-day engagement
- Audience demographics
- Traffic sources

Follower-Count to Engagement-Ratio

Overall, the *follower-count to engagement-ratio* refers to the number of likes and comments you have in relation to the number of followers. In your report, you should be able to see the content with the highest number of likes and comments. When evaluating this content, you need to know exactly what that content is. You must identify the similarities and differences between the content that is performing the best, which can often be the most subtle things. Ask yourself these questions: Is content that is performing best done with images that utilize the same camera settings, such as flash or no flash? Do videos perform better than static images? Does content with accompanying in-depth captions perform better than those without? Does content that features me and my image perform better than content in which I don't appear? Understanding the types of content that perform best will allow you to understand what types of content you should be posting. However, the reality of being a successful content creator is that not every piece of content you create will be high performing. Sometimes you'll need to create a type of content, whether for a brand or because you simply want to, that you know will not be optimal for engagement. The key here will be understanding what content *does* perform best, and utilizing that information to create an engagement-optimal content calendar, which will be discussed in the next chapter.

Time-of-Day Engagement

The time of day in which an influencer chooses to engage with their audience can be an incredibly effective metric in understanding post engagement. Depending on the platforms to which you post, as well as the primary location of your audience, there will be an optimal posting time for your content. This is the time of day when much of your follower base is active. This is incredibly important because posting in this window of time ensures that your content will be seen by most of your followers. For example, if you are based on the East Coast of the United States and the majority of your audience is based on the West Coast of the United States, it wouldn't make much sense to post your content at 9 a.m. EST, because that means that most of your audience is either asleep or engaged in early morning activities.

Demographics

Audience demographics are critical in determining who is interested in your content. Audience demographics can be used to help refine your audience and ensure you are attracting the types of people important to you. Audience demographics are important to understand for three reasons. First, they will determine what time of day to schedule your posts. Second, they will help you determine your language preferences. Finally, and most importantly, they will help shape the type of content you produce. For example, if you're based in India but most of your following is in the United States, you might want to consider English as your primary content language or have dual content languages available. As far as content is concerned, if you notice the majority of your audience is female, and that is your intended audience, you might want to tailor your content to that gender. Likewise, if you notice your audience is predominantly female but you have a desire to accumulate a more inclusive audience, you might start creating and promoting more content tailored to men.

Traffic Source

Understanding where your audience comes from will best help you increase your following on certain channels. Different platforms offer different data on traffic sources. Traffic sources define how users are interacting with your content. A large amount of traffic from a certain platform might be an indicator that your promotional efforts on that platform are successful, whereas low traffic numbers from different platforms might indicate that you could increase content engagement, exposure, or growth by increasing promotional efforts on that platform. For example, if you notice that a high number of visitors to your personal blog come from Instagram, yet almost none come from an organic search, this can indicate that your webpage visibility on Google is underperforming. To counteract this, you can explore multiple avenues, such as investing in Google Ads to promote your blog, optimizing your blog content for search engine optimization (SEO), or cross-promoting your blog on other social channels.

Within certain platforms, there are additional considerations to keep in mind regarding account exposure and growth. For example, with Facebook, exposure in people's newsfeed can be challenging. However, if you post regularly, comment on other pages, use images with your posts, reply to comments on your posts, tag other pages, and boost your posts, you will increase your visibility exponentially.

Instagram is much the same, but you will need to make sure that your content is high quality, and that you are posting content similar to your top posts. Be consistent in your posts, but don't over-post. You may get more engagement if you ask a question in your post captions. And be sure that you're using the right hashtags.

Twitter is a bit different. You will want to avoid too many hashtags, overwriting, over tagging, and too many self-involved posts. Plus, don't tweet just for the sake of tweeting. The key is understanding the platform with which you are interacting, and optimizing your posts based on what works best within each platform.

BRAND SPOTLIGHT

NATURA CULINA

Instagram: @naturaculina

Natura Culina is a wellness skincare brand promoting green and sustainable products and practices

Q: Do you work with influencers?

A: Yes. We have brand ambassadors, and we are constantly striving to collaborate with social media influencers.

Q: What percentage of your marketing budget/energy goes into Influencer Marketing?

A: It takes a big chunk of our time-schedule to plan and coordinate. I would say about 30 percent. As far as marketing costs, our ambassadors make a percentage of each sale with their ambassador code or influencer link.

Q: What is an example of a recent campaign that went well?

A: A recent campaign that was successful was a collaboration with our ambassador and product partner Morgan Tyler. Morgan hosted a "NC Day" on her page that resulted in her offering the following promotion—spend forty-five dollars and receive a free Rose'Berry Face Mask with your order when you apply code "roseberry" to your card. This campaign proved to be very successful.

Q: How do you vet influencers to ensure success?

A: We exercise a trial period with our influencers. We choose influencers who have a genuine connection to

Natura Culina so that they are transparent when promoting our brand. We send each individual our product to sample before offering them an opportunity to become one of our influencers. If they take to our products and want to join our team, we give them an influencer code or affiliate link to track their promotions and reward them through a commission on each sale.

Q: What are the benefits of working with influencers?

A: Influencers have a way of telling their version of the story that your brand represents. It's beautiful to see how each person takes to NC and how the brand has heightened and changed their lives. People get to see NC through each influencer's lens.

Q: Have you experienced a negative collaboration?

A: Yes, there is one collaboration where we received pushback. We collaborated with a small, woman-owned business that made handmade leather bags. Our vegan/cruelty-free followers did not support the idea of us promoting a company that sells leather goods. We learned that we have to be very careful and consider all angles of each collaboration.

This complete interview is available in Appendix F on page 230.

SUMMARY

Once you've reached nano-influencer status, you should be on the lookout for trends in your content that will allow you to optimize your account for maximum growth. Post engagement is key, so you will want to optimize your content to receive the most likes and comments. That's why every post you make, regardless of the platform, needs to be well thought out and valuable. Ask yourself, "Is this something I would like or comment on?" This way, you can keep your following/engagement ratio high, which will attract more brands and followers alike. Be sure that you're posting during high-traffic times for your followers. For example, if your audience is mostly mothers, you will want to avoid posting during dinnertime or children's bedtime hours. There are several ways to optimize your content. Each platform has its own rules and norms to follow, so it's important to fully understand the platform you are using before posting.

5. CONTENT STRATEGY

WITH EVER-CHANGING UPDATES TO SOCIAL-PLATFORM ALGO-rithms, it's more important now than ever to secure a solid content-strategy. An influencer's content strategy refers to the planning, development, and management of all content across all platforms. Being an influencer is a lot more than just posting every once in a while. Having a solid content-strategy will ensure that your account engagement remains steady and continues to grow. This means dedicating the time and effort to your audience and its interests, expectations, and schedules.

Plus, one of the greatest benefits to brands working with influencers is the unique development and delivery of their content. Together, influencers and brands can work as a team to create something incredible—just like Chrissy Teigen and BECCA Cosmetics did. Remember, influencers are also members of brands' target audiences, so collaboration on content is an excellent strategy.

GOALS

To begin defining a content strategy, you must first develop your content goals. These go hand in hand with your overall account goals but are a bit more specific. Your goal could be to create an aesthetically consistent feed, or to ensure that sponsored content and your original content are well spaced. It could also be something more methodical, such as making sure to organize content that historically performs poorly between content that is known to perform well.

Often, you will have more than one content goal, and that's okay. The tricky part will be staying on top of new content, new collaborations, and ensuring it is all organized in an effective way. The easiest way to start organizing content is to utilize a platform that lets you upload and organize on your own. For example, something like the app Preview should do the job as it allows you to upload content and captions, organize the photos as if they were featured on your Instagram page, and copy the caption out of the app when you're ready to post to Instagram. This is an easy tactic to use when you want to create an aesthetically cohesive feed.

BOOST ENGAGEMENT WITH CONTENT STRATEGY

A content strategy can be one of the most effective ways to alter account and content engagement. By defining which pieces of content perform well and which do not, you can effectively place poorly performing content behind highly engaging content. This will utilize the visibility and engagement of better performing content on the poorer performing content.

To understand how to boost engagement through a content strategy, you must first understand how your content is performing. To do this, you need to examine at least one month's worth of post data. You will need to consider metrics such as impressions, reach, and account size to determine the effectiveness of the content. Utilizing methods discussed in chapter 7, we will provide insight into how to effectively measure this data.

Once you have this data, you can begin to look for trends. Start by asking yourself a few basic questions:

- What are the similarities between my best performing content?
  - Does it share the same editing/lighting style?
  - What type of content is it? (e.g. selfie, flat lay, with friends, outside, in my office, etc.)
  - Was the post's caption engaging or a simple few words?
  - What kind of product or service was featured?
- What are the differences between my best performing content and worst performing content?

Once you have identified similarities between your best performing content and differences between your best and worst, you can begin to create a plan to minimize the effect of poorly performing content on your page. You might decide to not feature that type of content altogether, or you might want to change it to include similarities from your best performing content (e.g. better lighting, editing, or style of shot). However, you will often be faced with collaborations, products, and services that you know will not perform well. This is where a content calendar will help save your engagement.

While it will be entirely dependent on the contracts you have and the content you create, know that poorly performing content will perform better when placed after highly engaging and well performing content. The best method for holding onto engagement when posting something you know will perform poorly is to sandwich it between two pieces of highly engaging content.

When creating a content calendar, it can also be important to consider your audience demographics to determine the best day and time for posting. Once again, sample at least a month's worth of data to determine your highest engaging days, times, and location of the audience. This will help you understand when you should post. For example, if you are located in California, but the majority of your audience is based in NYC, it wouldn't make much sense to post late at night, as the content won't likely be seen by the majority of your audience.

CONSISTENCY AND FREQUENCY

Consistency is a huge part of developing an effective content-strategy. As you generate more content that performs better, you gain more traction, more content views, and more visibility to your account. This in turn boosts engagement of future content and overall account growth.

When starting out, you should determine a realistic number for how many pieces of content you aim to create each week. From that, you should plan for a content timeline around that set number of pieces. Keep in mind your best performing days and times. As you grow and decide to dedicate more time to your account, you should aim to post at least one piece of content every day to all platforms. To generate the most engagement on your content, you should ideally be generating at least one feed or static piece of content every day. Be sure to include supporting content via other methods or platforms (Instagram stories, Twitter posts, blog posts, etc.).

For example, influencers who are just starting out haven't yet completely committed to their account. So hypothetically the best they might be able to do is four static pieces of content each week. If they know that their best post days are Tuesdays at 12 p.m., and Thursdays at 9 a.m., then that will be the best time to post to maximize engagement. When planning your content strategy, you should plan to organize your content as:

- Best performing content on Tuesday at 12 p.m.
- Worst performing content on Wednesday.
- Best performing content on Thursday at 9 a.m.
- Additional content on Saturday.

With only four pieces of content, it's important to hit the times with high engagement, but be sure that not too many days of no posting go by. The more days that pass without posting, the more engagement will drop. It will be important to build momentum on days when engagement is high so that it can be sustained during times of no content.

BRAND SPOTLIGHT

BUKI

www.bukibrand.com

Instagram: @bukibrand

About Buki

Buki (boo-key) is a Seattle-based brand that specializes in luxury clothing sustainably crafted with state-of-the-art Japanese fiber technology, fabulous fits, and travel-ready comfort. Buki was co-founded by the husband-wife team of designer/entrepreneur Joey Rodolfo and marketer Stacy Bennett. Their men's and women's collections are exclusively crafted with their range of proprietary technical fabrics that provide fabrics that thermo-regulate to their collagen fabric, which softens and hydrates the skin. Buki is the Japanese word for "defend and protect," which is in reference to what the technical fabrics do for the wearer. The company is on trend with the rise of "ath-leisure" and "ath-lifestyle" clothing, as well as Wearable Wellness.

An interview with Stacy Bennett, co-founder and COO of Buki

Q: What do you look for in an influencer partnership?

A: We believe in win-win partnerships, where each party receives something of value. On our side, we look for great content that reflects the brand and tells our story in a photo. For the influencer, we look to provide a way for them to be an opinion leader and receive clothing as a thank-you for the partnership. We have several influencers that consistently deliver value for us, and we try to work with them as often as possible.

Q: How do you vet influencers to ensure success?

A: When looking at a new influencer that we haven't worked with before, I look for several key variables: Are they authentic and genuine? Are they reflecting their unique story in an authentic and genuine way? Then, I look at their audience size, but more importantly their engagement rate. Once those are a green light, I lay out the expectations clearly—from the look/feel/mood we're going for, to the timeline that we need the content to be delivered. Ninety percent of the time, everything goes smoothly. Once we find an influencer that is great to work with and they consistently deliver value, we build the relationship into an ongoing partnership.

Q: What characteristics of influencers do you look for (size, brand, demographics, style, etc.)?

A: We look at their audience size, engagement, if their look/feel/style/story is a fit with ours, and if their audience is consistent with ours.

Q: Do you have a story about a campaign that went badly?

A: Early into launching our brand, we worked with an influencer who provided us with her photos. We used them in our social content and a store marketing piece. We were contacted by the influencer's photographer, who insisted that those photos were her property and that we stop using them immediately. I reached out to the influencer to ask about it and she was taken aback as well. We discontinued using the photos and haven't worked with that influencer again either. I'm a big believer in giving credit where credit is due, and gave the photographer credit in the one to two uses of the photos. So in an abundance of caution, we simply stopped using the photos and didn't work with the influencer or the photographer again.

Q: What are the difficulties of working with influencers?

A: I've had an agreement with an influencer, sent them product, and they have never delivered content. They stop responding as well. It's not a good way of doing business, but it has happened to us a couple of times. It is the exception, not the rule, however.

Q: How do you find influencers? Do you use any Influencer Marketing platforms or agencies?

A: Because we are a startup with a small team, I rely on good, old-fashioned prospecting on IG. If I see someone that would be a good fit I reach out with a DM, or influencers will reach out to us via DM or EM. I haven't used any platforms or agencies—I think with a bigger program, those would have value, but for where we are now, it's working well.

This complete interview is available in Appendix F on page 226.

SUMMARY

To help boost your audience engagement, you will need to establish a content strategy, and that starts with developing your content goals. You will need to know how your content is performing, so you'll have to look at your trend analysis to help minimize the effect of poorly performing content on your page. Utilizing a content calendar will help you to determine the best days and times to post, keeping in mind the location of your most engaging followers.

How to develop a solid content strategy:

- Define your goals.
- Perform trend analysis & adjust as necessary.
- Post frequently (depending on platform norms).
- Post consistently.
- Post at high peak times for followers.
- Create a content calendar.

6. YOUR SOCIAL INFLUENCER MARKETING PLAN

FOR BRANDS

Before you can successfully utilize influencers on social media to build your brand and sell product, you must have a polished, cohesive, and effective social-media presence for your brand. A marketing plan can be a critical step towards successfully accomplishing this task.

If you are working for an existing company (as opposed to a startup), chances are, a social media presence already exists. In this case, it's up to you to evaluate your current state and create a strategy around moving your brand from where you are to where you need to be. If you are starting from scratch, you have a blank slate to establish your social-media presence. While this means you don't have any corporate bad habits or legacy situations to overcome, it also means you have zero momentum to build on.

A marketing plan designed to grow your social following could include any or all of the following:

Advertising plan: a promotion blueprint that provides the direction for companies and businesses to bolster sales.

Analytic tools and strategy: a blueprint to evaluate your marketing effectiveness. The strategy should include a plan to use analytic tools to measure effectiveness of the campaign.

Audience targeting: the process of targeting a specific consumer or demographic based on data to ensure marketing influencers are targeted in the right direction.

Brand outreach strategy: a strategy for the way that key messages are delivered to the target audience. A brand outreach strategy includes a number of methods by the influencer to ensure that the brand is top of mind for the audience.

Branding guidelines: a document that governs the look and feel elements of a brand. Brand guidelines often dictate how marketing collateral can be used.

Competitors: refers to a rivalry between two companies selling a similar product.

Content calendar: refers to the process of creating a calendar to push various content to gain competitive advantage in marketing.

Content types: video, picture, blog, etc.

Corporate structure: the various departments or business units that make up a company. Corporate structure is often dependent on the industry in which the company operates.

Current state analysis: a process by which a company documents current processes and procedures, typically with an eye on process improvement.

Differentiation factors: the process of creating special products that separate a business or organization from the competition.

Financing: the act of providing funding for marketing activities that will improve product position.

Goals: usually in Influencer Marketing, the goal is to promote user awareness of a product.

Ideal influencers to partner with: the process of identifying which social-media platforms to partner with to promote products.

Influencer partnering strategy: includes the ways in which you plan to use social media as a partner to promote your product.

Media kits: the kit that influencers bring to companies or brands for collaboration. A media kit consists of ways an influencer can help push a brand.

Mood board: a type of collage consisting of visuals, text, and sample objects that can convey a certain mood or idea.

Pricing sheet: typically, this is the price for hiring an influencer.

Profit plan: the plan to increase profits through an Influencer Marketing campaign. This is not always necessarily the goal.

Pro-formas: the methods by which companies or firms calculate financial results using certain presumptions.

While such a plan cannot guarantee success, as no plan can, it can give an influencer or brand a better chance for achieving their growth goals.

(See Appendix B on page 174 for an example Influencer Marketing plan.)

7. COLLABORATIONS

BRAND/INFLUENCER COLLABORATIONS ARE ONE OF THE MOST misunderstood components of social marketing from both perspectives. As an influencer, it is important to understand the fundamentals of this relationship to ensure you are properly compensated and set up for success. Similarly, as a brand, it is equally as important to ensure campaigns are effective with a positive return on investment. This way, your brand reputation is preserved, and you're making the most of your marketing budget.

Though it's possible to work with brands at any level, your offers for collaboration will be dependent upon your status as an influencer. For example, brands could offer influencers discounted product, free product, or money to promote their brands. That will directly correlate to the number of followers you have. For the most part, the following section is aimed at those who have more than 3,000 followers, as nano-influencers are more likely to simply sign up for an affiliate program on the brand's website than personally engage with anyone on a particular campaign.

Whether coming from the perspective of a brand or an influencer, you should consider the following factors of successful collaborations:

1. Finding brands or influencers to work with.
2. How to approach brands and influencers.

3. Types of campaigns.
4. Strategies for creating campaigns.
5. Mitigating your risks when working with brands and influencers.
6. Negotiating the best rates.
7. Protecting your investment with good contracts.
8. What to do if a campaign goes wrong.
9. Building performance measurement into your campaigns.
10. Compliance.
11. Having a pre-campaign checklist.

These factors of successful collaborations will be covered in greater detail over the next few pages.

FOR INFLUENCERS

Working with brands is the ultimate goal for most influencers. Even though influencers don't always receive a paycheck from brands, collaborations provide exposure and increase their working portfolio, which other brands can see. However, understanding how to begin working with brands can be a daunting task, as most influencers will likely lack a background in business operations and management.

To start, you can begin creating a portfolio of your most successful achievements. For example, there might be unique key performance indicators you can outline from some of your most successful posts, including likes, comments, and shares. Maybe you have been highlighted in media coverage or publications. Either way, it's important to document these achievements in a media kit (discussed in more detail below) or portfolio. That way, when you decide to pitch to brands, you have a starting point and you will look professional.

FOR BRANDS ══════

Depending on the type of brand, services, products offered, and marketing budget, working with influencers on social platforms could unlock a new channel for ultimate marketing performance. Influencer Marketing can produce a multitude of benefits for brands, including but not limited to:

- Increased brand awareness
- Emotional connection with audience
- Established trust with audience
- Increased sales
- Business development

Consider these three factors when determining if an influencer is an appropriate fit for your brand:

1. **Status and Image**

   Is status or image an important component of your brand? Influencer Marketing can be incredibly effective for brands that wish to promote or improve their perception. By utilizing influencers, you're giving a wide variety of faces to your brand. Everyday people promoting or being showcased using your products or services can easily impact brand reach and awareness. Influencers, especially micro-influencers, have a direct connection with their audience, which demonstrates trust. The audience trusts the influencer, and therefore is more likely to trust the brands the influencer promotes, compared to traditional advertising methods of the same brand or product. For example, more than 60 percent of consumers look to influencers to determine which products to purchase, and 81 percent of consumers turn to blogs for advice.[13]

2. **Competition**

Are you willing to face a lot of direct competitors? Influencer Marketing can be an effective marketing strategy for brands that operate in an over-saturated space. Through Influencer Marketing, you can create an emotional connection with your brand. By selecting an influencer who operates in the same niche as you, you can maximize their connection with their audience and your product to create an emotional and personal connection. In a recent study, it was shown that Influencer Marketing campaigns based on emotional content performed twice as well as campaigns based on intellect or facts.[14]

3. **Current Social Usage**

Are you already on social media? If your brand currently utilizes social channels as part of its strategy, it's likely that your name is already known through word of mouth, likes, shares, and follows. By utilizing Influencer Marketing, you can exponentially increase traffic leading back to your social channels, and therefore boost performance of such channels.[15]

---

13 Jessica Huhn, "Influencer Marketing Statistics That Prove Why It's So Popular," Business2Comunity, May 18, 2019, https://www.busiiness2community.com/marketing/influencer-marketing-statistics-that-prove-why-its-so-popular-02199795.

14 Harley Schachter, "20 Killer Examples of Influencer Marketing," Travel Mindset, https://www.travelmindset.com/20-influencer-marketing-examples/.

15 Sujan Patel, "How You Can Build a Powerful Influencer Marketing Strategy in 2020," Big Commerce, https://www.bigcommerce.com/blog/influencer-marketing/.

FINDING BRANDS OR INFLUENCERS TO WORK WITH

Once you've decided to pursue an Influencer Marketing strategy, you'll be tasked with finding the right influencers to promote your products or services. This can be one of the most difficult tasks for brands, because finding the right influencers will be critical to your social campaign performance. Finding the wrong influencers could be detrimental to your brand. In the world of social media, a scathing review by one well-trusted and well-connected influencer could set you back months.

To determine if an influencer is right for your brand, consider the following:

Niche

Do they operate in the same niche as you? Does your product fit within the bounds of their account? Not all brand/influencer relationships have to be a one-to-one match, but you should be cautious about approaching influencers well beyond the bounds of your services or products. For example, a brand that creates camping tents probably wouldn't want to approach an influencer who works in the beauty niche. Not only would the influencer likely not take the opportunity, but even if they did, their audience will unlikely be receptive to the brand's products. Always keep in mind the influencer's audience when making selections. To find influencers in your niche, try to avoid searching for "[Brand Niche] Influencers," as a lot of the articles that surface will be inaccurate or spam. Instead, search for influencers by looking at your competitors' pages and seeing who they have collaborated with. You can also search platforms like Instagram using hashtags. For example, if you're a clean-living brand you might search something like "#cleanhome" and then look at the most popular posts.

Followers

When selecting an influencer, you should consider their followers in conjunction with your marketing, campaign goals, and budget. For example, if you have a budget of $500 per influencer for a campaign, you'll be wasting your time looking at influencers with more than 100,000 followers. At this time, you should also check their follower health. There are loads of sites out there that will allow you to input an influencer's social handle to check the health of their followers. These sites will reveal the percentage of followers who are legitimate and those who are bots. Any influencer with more than 30 percent bots is not someone you want to work with. This means that they are likely purchasing followers to inflate their numbers. Note however, that as an influencer grows in followers, their number of inevitable bot followers grows as well, which is sometimes out of their control.

Engagement

Engagement is a critical evaluation criterion when selecting influencers. You'll notice that small influencers will likely have a larger engagement reach than large influencers. The typical engagement rate is anywhere from 4 to 12 percent. Anything lower than a 4 percent engagement rate is likely a waste of time, because this means their followers are not inclined to engage with them. An influencer with 20,000 followers and a 12 percent engagement rate could easily perform better than an influencer with 100,000 followers and a 5 percent engagement rate.

Reputation

Does your influencer have a reputation? Who are they? What are they really like? This can be a tricky evaluation criterion because social media is often a hostile place. Influencers are attacked by other influencers for the simplest of things, like purchasing the same jacket or using the same Adobe Lightroom preset. To gain the best perspective into influencer life and personality, follow them from a non-brand account and watch their stories on Instagram or their live videos. Influencers will often block brand accounts from viewing stories and live videos to prevent them from seeing their daily life or their true feelings about a brand or product. You should also consider evaluating an influencer's reviews about other brands and influencers. Are their reviews overly positive or absolutely scathing? You can tell a lot about an influencer based on how they speak not only of other brands, but also of others in the space. You should be mindful of red flags, as ultimately working with certain influencers can be damaging to your brand safety and reputation:

- Are they often caught up in social-media drama?
- Do they frequently cover controversial topics? (e.g., politics, religion, etc.)
- Do they promote illicit content? (e.g., alcohol consumption, drug use, etc.)
- Do they frequently use profanity?

Getting on a brand's PR list is one of the first indicators that your influencing is on the right track. It's the first sign that brands are recognizing the potential impact of your account and your audience. From there, you are more likely to be considered for affiliate marketing or sponsored opportunities. Getting on a PR list can be achieved both passively and actively, and you will see this differ within influencers based on the niche in which you operate. For example, you may find that many of the larger influencer accounts in the skincare niche will wait for brands to reach out to them, rather than actively seeking and reaching out to brands. Neither method is wrong. It comes down to personal initiatives and preference.

Influencers, especially micro-influencers, often fail to recognize two critical considerations. First, they tend to be oblivious to the oversaturation of influencers in any given niche and the amount of constant content on any given platform. Second, they tend to overlook how their follower engagement affects results. Because of this, many micro-influencers don't think they're ready to work with brands. They might feel that brands haven't reached out to them because they don't have enough followers or their content isn't good enough. Just remember, engagement is more important than followers, and market saturation is likely why brands aren't yet reaching out, as opposed to the content itself.

If you are an influencer with a high level of engagement, there is no reason to not reach out to brands that might be a good fit with your account. When reaching out to these brands you can approach them via email or social channels. In this case, social channels tend to be more responsive. Your message to the brand with whom you hope to work should include all the following information:

- Who you are
- What niche your account operates in
- Who your audience is (list any other relevant social channels you have)
- Your total number of followers across social platforms
- Your engagement rate

Providing your engagement rate is a critical component, as it will let brands understand the potential reach their products will have on your account. At this point you can even offer to send along post or story metrics showcasing your engagement.

- **Why you want to work with them**
  No brand enjoys receiving messages from influencers simply stating, "Hi! Love your products, can we collab?" It screams, "Give me free products." You should only reach out to brands you are genuinely interested in working with. Do research on the products or services they provide, and speak to them in the message you deliver. Talk about a recent launch they had, or something about their brand that personally speaks to you. Talking about something a brand has to offer shows them that you've already invested time and care in their brand.

- **What you can do for them**
  When reaching out to a brand for free products, you should keep in mind that they will want to know what you can do for them in exchange for these products or services. You could speak to how your audience responds to brands in the same niche, or you could state what you intend to do with the products or services. Make it personable, relatable, and something the brand will want.

An Example Message to a Brand That Sells Hair-Care Products:

Hi there!

My name is [Name] from [@Social.Handle], I am a beauty account and have been following your brand for a while now. I was very intrigued by your previous product launch of the sensitive hair-wash set, and I was hoping to work together in some capacity, as I have very thin and sensitive hair. I have around 20,000 followers right now, and my audience responds very well to reviews of hair-care products. They typically produce the highest engagement at 12 percent. I currently have 21,000 followers on Instagram and an average engagement rate of 10 percent. Across platforms, I have 45,000 average monthly viewers.

Please let me know if you would be interested in working together.

Thanks,

[Name]

Brand/Influencer Media Platforms

Becoming part of brand/influencer platforms is another method of introducing your product to an audience, or likewise, your account to prospective brands. There are various influencer media platforms, most requiring approval to join. But once approved, your opportunity for PR, sponsored collaborations, or revenue from affiliate rewards greatly increases.

- *Fohr*: Fohr is a membership network that connects brands with influencers. Fohr is especially targeted toward influencers that use Instagram because it can help them determine their audience demographics. www.fohr.com.
- *Octoly*: Octoly helps to connect influencers with brands to help create authentic content. www.octoly.com.
- *AspireIQ*: AspireIQ enables brands and influencers to work together to build the brands of tomorrow. www.aspireiq.com
- *Palm*: Palm is a matching service for like-minded brands and micro-influencers. www.joinpalm.com.

- *RewardStyle*: RewardStyle gives influencers exclusive access to a global network of 5,000 retail partners to help power the monetization of their content. www.rewardstyle.com.
- *SocialCert*: SocialCert tracks influencers' content and performance across platforms for each brand collaboration to help show how their content, likeness, and data are being used. www.socialcert.me.

MEDIA KITS

Once you've reached the point of sponsored or paid collaborations, brands will often ask for a media kit or a rate card. This is a document that will tell brands what services you provide and what you charge for each.

Your media kit should be a simple and visually descriptive one-page, living PDF document. It should be constantly updated and should include:

- Basic information—your name, social handle, location, links to all social channels, and contact information.
- A short description of who you are and what your account is about. Especially within PR agencies, your media kit may be passed around. So it's important to ensure that if it falls into the hands of someone that doesn't know you, there's enough information to give them an idea of who you are or what your account is for.
- Your metrics—how many followers you have on each relevant social channel, your engagement rate, and audience demographics. Audience demographics do not have to be in-depth, but should at minimum show where the majority of your audience is located and their genders.

- Services provided—in-feed posts, static content creation or photography work, video creation and types of videos (stop motion, YouTube, IGTV, etc.), giveaway posts, blog posts, story posts, etc. The types of services should also indicate which platforms they relate to.

- Rates for services—next to each service there should be a baseline price. You should list the minimum cost to create the type of content, and indicate an increase based on contract-specific requirements discussed in the next section, such as content usage, travel, or incurred fees, etc. This can be as simple as adding a "+" next to the price. Such as, "In-feed post: $500+."

- Date of creation—it is important to include the date of creation of the media kit, which can be done by simply adding a copyright footer or something similar to the bottom of your document. This is important because as your account grows, the metrics in your media kit will change, and subsequently so will your pricing. This will prevent brands from expecting the same rates despite your growing account (in the case of your media kit being passed around within an agency or brand).

Tip: many influencers choose to include specific post metrics as examples of engagement in their media kits. This can be beneficial as a selling point for brands when considering a collaboration. Oftentimes, most brands will be satisfied simply with the basic metrics listed above. Listing post-specific metrics can be tricky because it lengthens the document and requires more upkeep. It can also distort your perceived engagement because not all posts will perform the same. This can result in selling yourself short if your content performs better than the metrics listed, or it can lead to brand disappointment if your content underperforms based on the post metrics you provided. Post metrics should be left out of your media kit and only provided if a brand specifically asks for them.

Example Media Kit

The image on the next page is a sample media kit from Kate Fleming (@the.skincare.diary). Media kits can be as simple or comprehensive as needed by either the brand or influencer. The below media kit is an example of a simple media kit that shows basic metrics and rates for different kinds of services.

When brands are presented with an influencer's media kit, they should look for information to help determine if the influencer is the right fit for their specific campaign. This can be revealed through data, such as:

- Platforms they have a following on
- Rate or cost per engagement
- Account size for desired platform campaign
- Engagement rate

When evaluating media kits, keep in mind that often one or more data points may be inaccurate or inflated. Since media kits are living documents, they should be updated constantly as the influencer's account changes or grows. However, they can often be out of date. It is important to look at media kits in parallel with subsequent research on the influencer or utilization of an online tool that calculates and provides metrics on the influencer's account (examples include: Fohr, HypeAuditor, and Upfluence).

RATES

The next challenge influencers face in brand-influencer engagements is determining a price for the engagement type.

the
skincare
diary

ABOUT ME

I began my skincare journey in 2014 after
struggling with poor skin nearly my whole life.
This journey, as I began intense research and
product testing, quickly transformed into a
passion. In late 2017 I decided it was time to
share my passion with others.

BACKGROUND

I began my professional career in website
development and technology services and now
serve as an industry leader in digital analytics
marketing and engineering. This provides me
with a unique perspective and insight which I
apply to my own page allowing me to optimize
my engagement and increase ROI for myself and
collaborators through the powerful insights of
data.

ADDITIONAL SERVICES

Please ask me about my "Technical Media Kit" if you
are interested in any of these services:
• Brand Product Photography
• Custom Illustrations
• Website Development
• Guest Blog Writing
• Web or Digital Analytics Implementations

There really are no rules to follow or universal prices. The price is whatever the influencer and brand agree upon. Getting creative can be a great approach for both sides, especially on unique campaigns that don't fit the mold. However, the most typical engagement type is a sponsored post, and determining your influencer rate—what you charge brands—will depend on the following:

Following

How large of an account an influencer has is often indicative of how large of a reach they have. If you have a large following you will be able to charge brands more for sponsored work. The typical rule of thumb is fifteen dollars per 500 followers. For example, if you have 10,000 followers, your baseline rate should be $300 per post.

Engagement

Engagement also plays a huge role in determining your rate. With the number of deceptive social accounts and purchased followers, engagement is most important. Typical engagement rates are:

< 5 percent—Low

6–9 percent—Average

> 10 percent—High

Content Usage

Often brands will add in their contract parameters that outline the usage of content. If a brand intends to own full rights to the content that you produce, you should charge more. When brands own full rights to your content, this means your content can be used for anything the brand desires (e.g. photos for their website, emails, or other social campaigns). When determining your rate, you need to take this into account, because had this work been outsourced to a freelance photographer or content creator, it would likely cost twice as much, if not more, to produce.

If you have a higher engagement rate but a lower number of followers you will be able to tweak your rates to reflect that. For example, if you have 10,000 followers and a 15 percent engagement rate, take a look around your social channel for larger accounts that have the same number of likes and comments as you. You might find that with a 15 percent engagement rate, you are performing in the same category as other influencers who have a following of 50,000. Use the average follower number of accounts performing with the same like/comment ratio as you to determine your rates.

Paying influencers has often been a controversial topic. However, as Influencer Marketing progresses, one fact has become clear: brands must compensate influencers for ethical and reputational factors.

In many ways, influencers are just like any other channel of advertising. Until now, there has been an expectation that PR, exposure, increased traffic, and gifts alone were enough to compensate influencers, or incentivize them to post. That way of thinking is quickly fading. It wouldn't make sense to gift Google a bottle of shampoo and expect them to run an ad about it. So why should treating an influencer be any different?

Compensating influencers appropriately and fairly is important for a variety of reasons, from brand reputation to overall return on investment:

- Not all influencers will post your brand's product simply because you sent it to them—this is just a gamble and can result in a poor return.
- When you offer free product in exchange for exposure, you're sending the message that you don't value influencers' reach, craft, or time. You are essentially asking them to work for free, and you wouldn't dare expect the same from a television ad, for example. This can be considerably harmful to your overall brand image, as word will get out and other influencers may be put off from working with you altogether.
- You will get what you give—when influencers are appropriately compensated, they can churn out some of the most stunning pieces of content.

CONTRACTS

The most important piece of any influencer's brand engagement is the contract. The contract will protect both the influencer and the brand from any nuances or confusion. It should outline key points such as content usage, date of services, rates, and payment terms. At minimum, a contract should cover:

1. Dates
2. Content delivery dates
3. Posting, or go-live dates
4. Content requirements
5. Payment terms
6. Payment date
7. Payment type

However, the more information included in the contract, the better protected you are as a brand and as an influencer.

(See Appendix A on page 171 for a sample contract.)

In addition to the bare minimum listed above, contracts should also include information that will act to further protect and ensure the scope of the engagement:

1. Content specifications—Content specifications should be included in the contract, or at the very least, there should be a reference in the contract to a content brief or external document defining the types of content to be produced. The content brief should include a style guide as well as specific content requests on how the content should be produced to look. This should cover everything from the type of lighting required, to the type of files (RAW vs. edited), references to other brands, and everything in between.

2. Exclusivity—Exclusivity should state any other brands or services to be avoided during the dates of the engagement.

3. Deliverables—Deliverables are exactly what is expected of the influencer, penalties for late posting, and schedule of services if applicable.

4. Cancellation clauses—This could relate to non-performance, poor performance, breaking brand rule guidelines, etc., by either the brand or influencer.

5. Collateral details—What is considered approved content and briefing materials for the influencer?

6. Things to avoid—Is there anything specific the brand wants the influencer to avoid in their post?

7. Approval process—Will the brand want to see or approve the post before it goes live?

8. Confidentiality—A confidentiality clause states that the influencer can only share information that is relevant to the Influencer Marketing campaign.

9. FTC responsibility—It's important for the contract to state that it is the influencer's responsibility to comply with Federal Trade Commission (FTC) rules.

Aside from the minimum contract requirements, influencers should be especially aware of contact clauses, such as:

- Content Reshoots—When creating content for brands, especially with loose content guidelines, often brands will ask for a redo of content created. This can lead to many unplanned and uncompensated hours spent remaking content that has already been created. It is important to request that a reshoot clause be added into contracts that states compensation will be given in the event you must remake content. This will protect you from constantly having to redo content that otherwise appears within the guidelines. This will also encourage brands to create a thorough content brief.

- Late Payment—As an influencer, you should ensure that your contracts include a late payment clause. If a brand fails to pay you on time for the services you have already provided, you are entitled to additional compensation.
- Expenses—When working with brands, they may ask for work you cannot currently provide, such as specific lighting conditions, backdrops, locations, etc. If any work you intend to provide for the brand is not immediately accessible to you (e.g. causing you to travel or purchase a new backdrop) ensure that this cost is not coming out of your own pocket. Any additional materials needed to produce the content they are looking for should be discussed prior to the contract and should be fully detailed in the contract.

INFLUENCER SPOTLIGHT

KATY YATES

Maker, Sweet Littles Handmade

Instagram: @sweetlittleshandmade

Sweet Littles Handmade was founded in 2006 to fill a void in the children's stuffed-doll market. After struggling to find boy and gender-neutral dolls, we decided to make our own. Striving to create unique and very child friendly heirloom dolls for your babes, we create boy and girl dolls to meet all your snuggly needs.

Q: What's your number-one tip for brands looking to engage an influencer?

A: Know your customer. There is nothing more ridiculous than having a brand reach out that clearly hasn't even looked at your profile. When a brand reaches out that my following wouldn't connect with it is a waste of my time and theirs, and none of us have time for that.

Q: Who do you like to work with and why?

A: My favorite is working with people and brands that are just starting. That's when I can see my influence the most. When I make a post and their business blows up, or if I can help pair them with an influencer who can do that for them, those are the people I want to surround myself with.

This complete interview is available in Appendix E on page 195.

8. CREATING A SUCCESSFUL INFLUENCER MARKETING CAMPAIGN

PLANNING YOUR INFLUENCER CAMPAIGNS AND BUILDING AN overall marketing plan is a good practice to improve your success. Keep in mind that utilizing influencers doesn't only need to be restricted to social media. You can leverage an influencer's audience in many ways. Besides posting content on Instagram, YouTube, Pinterest or the like, many unique and creative methods of utilizing influencers are available to you. These can include:

- In-store events
- Television
- Sporting events
- Magazines
- Film screenings
- Concerts
- Benefit events

- Audiobooks
- Podcasting
- Packaging
- Email
- Text messaging
- Your own brand app
- Product design
- Blogging

Once you have decided on your campaign, channel, and overall concept, it's time to plan the campaign, considering the following factors:

- Identification of multiple influencers who you would like to target for the campaign
- Strategy for how to win the relationship of your choice (how are you going to get their attention?)
- Template emails, DMs, or other outreaches that you will use to solicit influencers
- Contract and terms of the campaign
- Budget for the influencer and all other components of the campaign
- Goals
- Key metrics and a plan for analysis. How will you be sure of the return on investment for this campaign? What is a win?
- Press kit to entice influencers to work with you
- Identification of any unique perks of the project to win the best influencer you can find

Spending the necessary time to plan ahead of your campaign will make a huge difference in its overall success. Not only that, but when you have a plan ahead of time, you can evaluate the effectiveness of your campaign. This can help you become more realistic about your expectations going forward. It can also help you to be more disciplined in executing your campaign according to best practices. Chapter 8 provides greater detail around building a successful campaign, from choosing which campaign is right for you, to how to avoid pitfalls and mistakes. To begin, let's review a few of the most common types of campaigns.

TYPES OF CAMPAIGNS

In this new age of Influencer Marketing there is no set standard for how brand and influencer campaigns work. Most influencers do not have a background in marketing or business, and that's OK, but that often leads to confusion about how the engagement should operate. Many different kinds of campaigns are possible, some of which were mentioned in the previous section. However, five kinds of campaigns are most common. These will be reviewed in greater detail over the following pages.

PR

One of the most common questions asked by micro-influencers relates to PR. PR simply stands for public relations, but in the arena of influencer-brand relationships, PR is often associated with a brand offering an influencer a gift of free products or services. Of course, nothing is *free*. Brands do this in the hopes that the influencer will share it on their social channels, thereby generating brand awareness. PR is almost always considered a gift. Influencers are not obligated to post PR products or services. If posting is a requirement of receiving PR, then it is technically considered payment rather than a gift. This is because the product/service holds monetary value, and you are required to comply with Federal Trade Commission (FTC) regulations, as well as disclose this on your income tax statements.

As a brand, utilizing PR to attract potential consumers through influencers can be an incredibly effective and low-cost strategy. Providing PR to influencers is essentially gifting them products or services in the hopes that they promote them, therefore generating brand awareness and visibility to your brand's page.

Often, brands approach PR as an exchange. For example, in exchange for their gifts of product, they expect a social post or mention in return. It should be noted that gifting in exchange for a post (or anything) is not a gift, and both your brand and the influencer must adhere to FTC standards and disclose the exchange.

Sponsored Posts

Sponsored posts are when an influencer and brand enter into an agreement that states the influencer shall post (or meet other campaign criteria) and in turn will be compensated for doing so. To comply with FTC regulations, these types of engagements require disclosure upon posting. This is where you will typically see "#ad" or "#sponsored" under the post. It is important to note that a collaboration can be considered a sponsored engagement even if the influencer is not being paid directly. Asking an influencer to post in exchange for receiving a free product is still considered an exchange of monetary value and is still subject to FTC compliance.

Content Creation

Sometimes brands will seek the work of influencers to create content that won't be posted on the influencers' social channels. Perhaps you're an influencer who takes stunningly beautiful photographs. A brand might see this and want to use your services to create images for their brand or to use in their marketing portfolio.

Competitions and Giveaways

Running giveaways on social channels can be one of the easiest and cheapest ways to gain brand awareness, depending on the price point of your products or services. Tip: invoke giveaway rules that require the audience to follow both the influencer and the brand, as well as a requirement that states each entry should only be considered valid if a comment is left tagging friends. This will not only incentivize the influencer to participate in the campaign by guaranteeing exposure to their account, but will also provide extended reach to the brand account via association.

Discount Codes and Affiliate Marketing

Utilizing discount codes can be one of the most effective ways to track return on investment within influencer campaigns. Most discount codes or affiliate links will contain a unique code or URL that is easily measurable. Affiliate campaigns are also often a more cost-effective form of Influencer Marketing. In this case, the influencer is only given a small percentage of total profit conversions from their unique code, rather than a lump sum payment for a one-time promotion. Discount codes give an influencer the opportunity to generate as much or as little of their own return on investment as they want. For example, the more they promote a product and drive their audience to convert, the more they are compensated. In turn, this often generates more brand awareness and conversions. This is because the product or services are continuously promoted, versus a one-time promotion, often seen in a standard PR or sponsored engagement.

Engagement and Impressions

When approaching a brand for a collaboration, it's important to keep up to date with what they are looking for. For example, follower number is no longer the only, or even the primary, metric brands evaluate when considering an influencer. When approaching a brand for a collaboration, you should clearly communicate your engagement rate by stating the following:

- Your account followers for a given platform—typically the platform from which you are contacting them, or the platform on which you hope to collaborate with them.
- Your brand followers—a holistic monthly average of the number of people who see your content across platforms (blog views via an analytics service such as Google Analytics, Instagram followers, Pinterest viewers, etc.).
- Your engagement rate of a given platform—if you're hoping to collaborate on Instagram, share your Instagram engagement rate (to calculate engagement rate refer to the methods in chapter 9).

Even with a smaller number of followers, your engagement rate will tell brands the return on investment they can expect from collaboration with you. By providing a holistic brand following, you're increasing your chances of a collaboration. Although the brand may not have the budget or need for a specific platform collaboration, they may have space for you in a different vertical or a campaign across another platform. Providing your engagement rate will also affect the pricing of your collaboration.

A Few Final Thoughts on Campaigns

Selecting influencers for a campaign isn't easy. Brands should take into account a multitude of factors and should emphasize an influencer's engagement within their platform from a measurable perspective. Engagement will help determine the budget offered to influencers as well as the expected return from the influencer for any given campaign. The engagement rate should be closely examined to determine the authenticity or health of the influencer's account and following.

Creating a social campaign utilizing Influencer Marketing can be established both prior to and after selecting influencers, and there are benefits on both sides. There are multiple factors to take into consideration, which are ultimately a direct reflection of defined business metrics. To begin creating a campaign you must first identify the following:

1. Campaign goals—Are you hoping to increase brand awareness, generate revenue from a specific product or service, compete with a competitor's product launch, etc.? Determining your campaign goals will aid in the process of selecting influencers, developing a campaign schedule, and identifying key performance indicators for determining the success rate of your campaign.

2. Budget—Determining your campaign budget will go hand in hand with your campaign goals and influencer options. If your primary campaign goal is to create brand awareness, you might not have a budget or offer compensated work aside from the actual products or services themselves. However, if you had a higher budget for a brand awareness campaign, that means that you'd likely be able to approach larger influencers, and in turn, a larger audience. Budget will dictate the type of campaign you can run, as well as the class, or size, of influencers you can approach.

3. Platform—Deciding on a platform will be determined by the content your campaign desires, or the type of influencer. Certain content performs better on certain platforms. For example, stunning photographs will perform best on platforms like Instagram, whereas highly

engaging short video clips will perform better on Facebook. When deciding on your desired content, keep in mind that you will want to target influencers who produce the same type of content.

Once your campaign goals and budget have been determined, you can begin the process of defining KPIs and selecting influencers. If you are defining your campaign based on the influencers your brand wants to approach, that's fine too. Not every campaign must follow strict content schedules.

COMPLIANCE AND WHEN CAMPAIGNS GO WRONG

FOR INFLUENCERS

Your first collaboration with a brand will be a new and exciting experience. It's often easy to overlook the details in the excitement of your new opportunity, but it's important to understand that not every collaboration will go as planned. Not all collaborations will be successful or respectful, and some will even leave a bad taste in your mouth. It is solely your responsibility to understand every aspect of the collaboration before agreeing to or signing a contract:

- What is the scope of work?
  - What are you agreeing to in relation to the contract and deliverables?
  - What is the language to be delivered?
  - What are the timelines?
- Who is the brand?
  - Are they well respected?
  - Do they have a good reputation amongst the community?

- Ask around within the community or niche you operate in to get a holistic view of the brand.
- Do the services or products align with your account?

Common pitfalls of brand/influencer collaborations:

- The brand asks for content within a timeline that is not feasible.
- The brand asks for a review of a product that doesn't align with your account.
- You are held to using post-caption language that you don't believe in.
- You discover the brand has a bad reputation and no longer want to associate yourself with it.
- The contract wasn't specific enough, and the brand asks for content reshoots or additional content for which you are not compensated.
- You discover that you have priced yourself well below what the brand is offering to other influencers.

Terminating a campaign:

This can be tricky because legally you are bound to the language and requirements set forth in your contract. This is why it is incredibly important to thoroughly read your contract prior to signing it. Also, it is critical to research and become familiar with all aspects of the brand and its products before executing a contract.

It's inevitable, though, that at some point in your influencer journey something will slip through the cracks, or something will come up that causes you to become unable to fulfill the requirements. Maybe you discover shortly after signing the contract that the brand is not one you want to be associated with. Or, the contract wasn't specific enough to include the exact product or services that you will be promoting, and they don't align with your account. Maybe you have a family emergency and you are unable to hit the deliverable deadlines.

The first step in mitigating a campaign issue or miscommunication is to determine if you want to proceed with the collaboration. If the answer is yes, then:

- Ask—Can the deadline be extended? Can you review a different product or service? Can you move your deliverables to a different platform?
- Explain—Behind every brand is a person. More often than not they are accommodating and understanding that life happens, and sometimes things come up that are out of your control. By providing an explanation you give them reasons to better understand your position and why you need the things you are asking for.

Sometimes the issues you face in collaboration will be beyond mitigating. You may find yourself wanting to terminate the collaboration. Legally legitimate reasons for campaign termination include:

- Product/services sent late, so that the timeline cannot be met.
- Post-caption language requested that was not specified in the contract.
- Change of posting platform.
- Change of fees.
- Requests for content reshoots.
- Brand asks for you to not disclose the sponsorship.

Other legitimate reasons for terminating a collaboration, that are not within legal reasons:

- Emergencies preventing completion of the contract within a timeline.
- Discovering the brand is not one you want to be associated with.
- Inability to fulfill the contract to the best of your abilities for whatever reason.

Illegitimate reasons for ending a collaboration:

- You priced yourself too low and now no longer want to do the work at the current rate.
- You changed your mind about the scope of work or don't want to adhere to the posting requirements.
- You accepted a collaboration that was an exchange of a product or service for a post, and now you don't want to post.

When deciding to terminate a contract, you must ensure your reason for cancellation is at the minimum legitimate. It's OK if it's not a legally binding reason, as long as it is not something as illegitimate as deciding you don't want to do it anymore. When cancelling for a legally legitimate reason, you should ensure you are paid for your work or services delivered up to the point of cancellation. If cancelling for any other legitimate reason, you should ensure that you are either paid if the brand wants what you have delivered so far, or that they will not be utilizing your content in any way moving forward.

When cancelling a collaboration, remember to remain respectful and to not burn bridges unless absolutely necessary. The social advertising management space is a small world, and often you will encounter these same people and agencies in the future. Plus, they may have other collaboration opportunities available for you, or they've moved on to other brands. You will want to leave as many doors open as possible for long-term success. Protecting your reputation is critical for future success, as some brands may want to work with you again.

FOR BRANDS

Terminating a collaboration from a brand perspective is a process much like an influencer cancellation. There also must be legal or legitimate reasons, as mentioned above. Cancellation for illegitimate reasons will give your brand a bad reputation, and other content creators may not want to work with you as a result.

The most important thing to take into consideration when cancelling a collaboration with an influencer is payment for services/content already delivered. If an influencer has already provided one round of deliverables, they must be paid for the work completed at a prorated cost of their original contract payment. Even if they have only provided one round of content for approval or revisions, that is still work provided that they had to create. It was still time spent on your brand, for which they should be compensated.

During an influencer/brand collaboration, you might find that an influencer's style, work, etc., was not what was expected. This is why it is equally as critical for brands to research influencers as it is for influencers to research brands. Because of this, it is also critical to always add a revision clause to your contract. This will help you to better clarify your expectations of the content moving forward.

A NOTE FROM KATE (@THE.SKINCARE.DIARY)

In my time as a content creator, I have cancelled only two collaborations after signing the contract. There was one particular collaboration I cancelled because

I didn't feel right promoting the products in any way. I could have continued the collaboration and written a negative review, but in my mind, any press, positive or negative, is still press. I ultimately didn't want to push this brand out to the world. I also didn't want to be associated with them in any way. I had originally jumped into the collaboration after doing some research on the brand and the products. I was feeling good about both. However, it had only come to my attention after speaking with a friend that the brand was actually owned by a hard pushing multi-level marketing (MLM). From prior internet research alone this never came to light, and I was only able to find the connection after learning about it and specifically searching for it. When terminating my contract, I had not yet done any work for the brand. I simply and respectfully reached out stating my ask, and my explanation:

"Hey there, I apologize for the turnaround, but after some further research into these products and this collaboration I realized I don't think this would be a good fit for me, my account, or audience. I was wondering if it would be possible to terminate my contract. Again, apologies for this last minute decision."

The brand was bummed and said they were sorry to hear that. However, they were completely understanding, and that was that. I've found that if it's been made aware to a brand that you don't want to work with them, they won't push for it, as they want someone who is excited about them and their products. The best thing you can do as a brand or influencer to mitigate risk in collaborations is ensure you've done adequate research on the brand, the influencer, the products or services, and the language and requirements of your contract, ensuring that the contract is as specific as it can be.

PRE-CAMPAIGN CHECKLIST

Prior to accepting a campaign, influencers should ensure that they can meet the expected requirements. These questions will help you to determine if the campaign is right for you:

1. Do I believe in the brand and the product (or services)?
2. Do I believe in or agree with the work I am being asked to do?
3. Do I have the resources available to complete the proposed scope of work?
4. Does the campaign fit within my schedule? Will I have adequate time to complete the proposed work?

Once the campaign goals and budget have been established, and your brand has a rough list of influencers to reach out to, the next step will be determining if they meet your campaign criteria. When approaching an influencer for a campaign, be sure to check that they meet all criteria of the campaign, including:

1. Budget—Are they within your budget? When negotiating with an influencer, it's best to be up-front about the cost of the engagement. It's frustrating for both sides to go through the process of back and forth emails about the nuances of an engagement, only to find out in the end that the budget does not align. On top of that, influencers talk—especially to one another. You don't want to discover that you've put your brand in a bad position by being deceitful about the true cost of your influencer campaign budget.

2. Timeline—If your campaign has a schedule, ensure upfront that the influencer has the availability to meet the campaign deadlines.

3. Non-Compete—Prior to the start of any contract, your brand should check for any non-compete or exclusivity work in the current influencer's portfolio. This will prevent the influencer from doing any last minute cancellations.

4. FTC Compliance—Believe it or not, there are influencers out there who refuse to comply with FTC regulations. Make sure your influencers know that if they are to be compensated for the campaign, they must comply with FTC regulations.

5. Work Eligibility—If based in the United States and offering compensation for an engagement, you should always guarantee that your influencer is eligible to work in the United States.

BRAND SPOTLIGHT

WYLDE LINGERIE

www.wyldelingerie.com

Instagram: @wyldelingerie

About Wylde Lingerie

Wylde is a Seattle-based, women-owned lingerie brand born out of love for lingerie and all things romantic. Their intimates bring together a touch of love, lust, and romance, and their mission is to celebrate women by providing an intimate layer for self-expression while cultivating femininity and empowerment. They believe in enhancing a woman's body without the need to change anything, and think of their pieces as love potions, for self love and all other loves.

An interview with co-founders Vera Burgos and Romina Serrate

Q: What percentage of your marketing budget/energy goes into Influencer Marketing compared to your other forms of marketing?

A: About 35 percent.

Q: Share an example of a recent campaign that went well.

A: We partnered up with ten influencers for our latest summer capsule. Each influencer produced content showcasing our new pieces to be featured in our Instagram page. The content we received was unique. Each influencer created what they felt would resonate with their audience, and we loved that variety. The creative freedom allows for the content to feel authentic. It also encourages our customers to have fun and tap into their artistic side to post their pictures with our product to be featured too.

Q: How do you measure campaign success?

A: We mostly measure success by tracking key performance indicators like influencer promo codes, email sign-ups, reach, impressions, engagement, and website traffic.

Q: Do you have any examples of campaigns that didn't work out the way you hoped?

A: Our first influencer campaign was a learning experience in that out of fifteen influencers we chose to work with for the product release, two didn't deliver. From this we learned how to better assess the influencers we partner with. Now we also intentionally schedule a few exchanges with them prior to the agreement to get a feel for their level of commitment. It doesn't mean that it won't happen again, but we are taking measures to ensure that we can improve and continue to build meaningful partnerships.

Q: What are the primary benefits you receive from campaigns (e.g. photos, exposure, sales, affiliation with an influential person, etc.)?

A: Content and brand awareness. Content is costly to produce, and branding takes time. Influencer Marketing helps us with both of these.

Q: Do you require ownership of copyright for content?

A: Yes, it is part of our influencer agreement.

Q: How do you go about creating a campaign (do you let the influencer run with it, do you have a team that creates the concepts, etc.)?

A: Once we have chosen who to work with, we trust their creative process. A good influencer knows what resonates best with their audience. This circles back to the influencers knowing who follows them, and consistency of posting and content on their feeds.

Q: What is the most important key to success in Influencer Marketing in your opinion?

A: To focus on choosing the right influencers for a campaign. They will be the face of the brand, so it is important that their values are in sync, in my opinion.

This complete interview is available in Appendix F on page 221.

SUMMARY

Your first collaboration with a brand will be a new and exciting experience. As such, it's often easy to overlook the details of the collaboration. However, it's important to protect yourself and ensure you are not being taken advantage of. The checklist below will help to remind you of some key points to consider before entering into a brand collaboration or contract. You will want to ensure that:

- You fully understand the scope of work (including all specifics, reshoots, etc.).
- Timelines are reasonable.
- You are being compensated appropriately.
- The product aligns well with your account.
- The wording aligns well with your account.
- The product will speak to your audience.
- The brand is well respected.
- You have fully read and understand the contract.
- The contract is comprehensive and protects both the influencer and brand.
- There is a termination clause.

Just remember, not all collaborations will go as planned. However, it's important to remain respectful and to not burn any bridges. The Influencer Marketing space is small and neither brands nor influencers want to get a bad reputation before they even start.

9. CAMPAIGN METRICS AND ANALYTICS

FOR BRANDS

Marketing is part art, part science. Since marketing is entirely based on humans communicating with humans, there are very few cut-and-dry best practices. What works in one context may not work in another. However, one universal aspect of marketing is the need to approach it with an iterative expectation. For example, your first campaign might be highly successful, but you may struggle after that and have to focus on improving your results over time. This is why measuring is so important. Without measurement it's impossible to know what requires improvement or the effects of the changes you make. To help guarantee a successful influencer campaign, your brand must have the ability to measure its performance. A well-executed campaign needs to take most or all of the following into consideration:

- Sales
- Content impressions
- Audience reach
- Ad clicks
- Increase in brand followers

- Content engagement
- Content views

Evaluating these key performance indicators against each other will allow your brand to evaluate the overall performance of the campaign as well as the performance of the individual influencers. For example, comparing the number of all content views across all influencers in the campaign versus the number of click-throughs will be a good indicator of the number of people driven to take action on the content. This will give you a percentage of the number of people who saw your content and converted. A higher percentage indicates a more successful campaign. On the same note, evaluating those criteria on the individual influencer scale will be indicative of how the individual influencer performed within the campaign.

HOW AND WHAT TO MEASURE

Good marketers live and die by the numbers. Key performance indicators are established ahead of time and are most critical to achieving a return from a marketing strategy. To effectively measure KPIs, they must be broken down into primary and secondary metrics.

Primary metrics consist of organic platform KPIs such as:

- Likes
- Comments
- Post impressions
- Post reach
- Post shares
- Video views
- Post saves

Secondary metrics consist of off-channel, lower-funnel customer behavior such as:

- Traffic to a website
- Sales/purchases
- Email subscriptions
- Add to cart
- Downloads

Primary Metrics

Identifying winning campaigns on-channel involves a cross analysis of primary metrics. You may want to evaluate the success of on-channel campaigns if you are trying to measure the effectiveness of the platform against others, the effectiveness of a particular influencer, or influencers in general, within a social channel. Measuring primary metrics is beneficial if your campaign goals include brand awareness, content views, increased audience, etc., which are typical goals of young or indie brands.

A SAMPLE REPORT:

In this example, assume the influencer campaign was completed utilizing five influencers on Instagram. Their requirement was to create and post two static pieces of content over one month's time. The goal of the influencer campaign was to generate brand awareness and content views.

To measure the effectiveness of a campaign, you will need access to the social-media metrics, which the owner of the account can provide. Most often, this comes in the form of screenshots. This requirement should be listed in your contract with the influencer. This will give you the number of likes, comments, saves, shares, post reach, impressions, and website clicks.

Once you have the content metrics, you can calculate the post-engagement rate using this simple formula:

[comments] + [likes] = [total engaged]

[total engaged] / [number of followers] x 100 = [engagement rate]

You can utilize this engagement rate or the average engagement rate of an influencer's campaign posts in comparison to the engagement rate they provided in their media kit (media kits discussed in chapter 7). This will not only determine if it is accurate with what they have provided, but also whether your campaign was successful on their channel. If their engagement on your campaign post performed more than 3 percent less than their typical engagement rate, you can assume your campaign was not the best fit for them. While many factors can affect post engagement, and it is true that most sponsored posts inevitably perform worse than an influencer's organic content, it is the brand's responsibility to determine the threshold engagement percentage that will signify a successful or unsuccessful campaign.

Using the same example, we can dig deeper within the metrics to try and understand why a post was successful or not. While no one understands for certain how the Instagram algorithm works, it is well known that posts that receive high engagement in the first half hour tend to perform better than those that don't, simply by boosting reach and impressions. When looking at reach, we can compare the metric to post engagement as well as the total number of the influencer's followers. If the influencer has 100,000 followers and their reach on the campaign post was 20,000, that means that only about 20 percent of their following saw the post (factoring in percentage of accounts reached that weren't already following).

Without understanding exactly how the Instagram algorithm works, it's hard to say for certain why their reach was what it was. Perhaps the content didn't truly speak to the audience. Maybe it wasn't eye-catching enough. Or, perhaps it was posted at the wrong time of the day and didn't gain the initial traction necessary. Maybe Instagram had just made another update. Nonetheless, knowing which influencers have a high reach with your content will be incredibly valuable. This is not only for future campaign considerations, but also in the event that your brand wants to take influencer campaign marketing to the next level by placing ad spend behind well-performing influencers, or by utilizing tracking URLs and redeveloping campaign goals to include revenue or sales performance.

Ultimately, it's difficult to gain any concrete opinions on an influencer's performance from simply one post. So, to best measure an influencer's performance, you should measure at least three pieces of content over a month's period.

Secondary Metrics

Measuring secondary metrics often relates to campaign goals of increased sales, subscriptions, downloads, or other off-channel conversions. When choosing influencers for these types of campaigns, brands should consider good performance based on the measurement of the primary metrics above.

When measuring an influencer or group of influencers in relation to performance on campaigns that utilize secondary metrics, it is critical that tracking solutions are put in place prior to the start of the campaign. Things like custom URLs and unique promo codes need to be considered.

Utilizing unique promo codes will allow you to see the total number of conversions that are a direct result of a particular influencer. Utilizing unique URLs will also give you this insight, as well as any other online actions deemed relevant by your campaign goals. If you are utilizing unique URLs, your ability to measure online user actions will be reliant on your current digital analytics implementation (such as Google or Adobe Analytics).

To calculate the success of an influencer campaign containing these secondary metrics, your brand should take into account the engagement and reach from the social content, the engagement with the call to action (swipe-ups from story posts, website clicks, etc.) and the total number of conversions utilizing the unique tracking method.

A SAMPLE KPI REPORT:

For this example, assume that the influencer campaign has utilized five influencers on Instagram. Their requirement was to create and post one static Instagram post. This post included language driving followers to the link in their bio to utilize their unique promo code, and one story post that included a swipe-up link to the brand's website and their promo code. The goal of the influencer campaign was to drive users to the brand's website and generate sales.

The first step in assessing the success of this campaign is to determine the reach of the static post and the Instagram story. This can be done by requesting the post and story metrics from the influencer. The next step will be to determine, of those reached, how many converted on the call to action. Again, this can be done by requesting metrics from the influencer. Lastly, you will want to look at the number of times their unique promo code was used on your website. Combining these numbers will give you a general conversion rate for both the social-channel performance as well as off-channel performance:

[story views] + [post reach] = [total reach]

[website clicks (from post)] + [link clicks (from stories)] = [total call-to-action (CTA) conversion]

[total CTA conversion] / [total reach] x 100 = [social-conversion rate percent]

[number of promo uses] / [total CTA conversion] x 100 = [off-channel conversion rate percent]

To better illustrate this, let's input real numbers:

[8,000] + [125,000] = 133,000

[250] + [500] = 750

750/133,000 x 100 = 0.56 percent social-conversion rate

750/110 x 100 = 14.6 percent off-channel conversion rate

Understanding these formulas and their output will help to identify successful and unsuccessful campaigns in two areas: on the influencer's social channel and on your digital platform. A low social-conversion rate could be explained by poor content performance or methods explained in primary metric analysis in the above section. Alternatively, a low off-channel conversion rate could be indicative of many things that must be explored further via a digital-analytics solution. These can include:

- Critical website issues or errors especially in the checkout funnel
- Too-high cost of shipping
- Improper product placement
- Ineffective website flow

These can be explored by many methods, such as:

- Customer journey analysis
- A/B testing
- Cart abandonment analysis
- Customer feedback
- Survey analysis

This can all be done with a digital-analytics tool and measurement strategy.

TOOLS YOU SHOULD BE AWARE OF TO HELP YOU TRACK KEY PERFORMANCE INDICATORS AND IMPROVE YOUR PERFORMANCE

Fortunately, there are nearly unlimited tools available to influencers and brands who want to quickly and effectively track and understand key metrics. This section describes some of the most popular and important tools for you to consider as part of your KPI tracking process.

KPI Tracking Tool	Price	Description
Google Analytics	Standard Version: Free Premier Version: $150K	Uses JavaScript to collect information about website, including site visits, etc.
Crazy Egg	$24 per month	Heat-mapping software that will tell you where the user spends their time on websites.
Followerwonk	$79 per month	Helps users dig deeper into their Twitter following to understand who their followers are.
Brandwatch	Pro Version: $1000 per month	A company in the UK that sells three products, including Consumer Research, Audiences, and Vizia. All of these products help companies monitor their social-media presence.

Mixpanel	Starts at $999 per year	Tracks user interactions with web and mobile applications. Provides tools for targeted communications with these applications.
BrandMentions	Starts at $49 per month	Monitors the number of times a brand is mentioned on the internet.
Sprout	Professional license: $149/month Advanced license: $249/month	Finds people who love your brand through social interactions.
Meltwater	Basic package $10–25/month Extensive apps $100/month	Software as a service that monitors brand performance compared to the competition.
Fohr	Does not provide public pricing	Membership network that connects brands with influencers.
TapInfluence	Does not provide public pricing	Provides three levels of Influencer Marketing software.
Agorapulse	Small company: $79/month Large company: $159/month Extra-large company: $239/month Enterprise: $399/month	Social-media management software that helps companies drive engagement and moderate social-media mentions.

Hootsuite	Professional: $29/month	Social-media management platform.
	Team: $129/month	
	Business: $599/month	
	Enterprise: (custom pricing)	
Tailwind	$9.99/month (paid annually) $15/month.	Helps companies save time by optimizing the time for posts on Instagram and Pinterest.
NetBase	Basic: up to $200/month	Social-media analytics company that helps businesses collect data from social media.
	Extensive: $300–$1,000/month	
Keyhole	Professionals: $199/month	Tracks hashtags on Twitter, Instagram, and Facebook.
	Corporations: $599/month	
	Agencies & Enterprises: $999/month	

SUMMARY

A well-executed marketing campaign needs to take into consideration sales, content impressions, audience reach, click-throughs, increase in brand followers, content engagement, and content views. To effectively measure key performance indicators, they must be broken down into primary and secondary metrics. Primary metrics consist of organic platform KPIs, such as likes, comments, post impressions, post reach, post shares, video views, and post saves. Secondary metrics consist of off-channel, lower funnel customer behavior, including traffic to a website, sales/ purchases, email subscriptions, add to cart, and downloads.

Ultimately, it's difficult to gain any concrete opinions on an influencer's performance from simply one post. So to best measure an influencer's performance, you should measure at least three pieces of content over a month's period.

10. ETHICS AND THE DARK SIDE OF SOCIAL MEDIA

FOR INFLUENCERS

As hard as it is to become an influencer, remaining one and continuing to grow is even more challenging. Once you begin micro-influencing thousands of followers (3–20K), you'll begin to realize just how demanding and time consuming this "hobby" really is. This is when you must bear down and do what it takes to become a successful influencer. That means influencing will now become a full-time job for you. You'll begin to discover the nuances and hidden inner workings of what it really means to be a known persona on social platforms. That means you have to learn how to take the bad with the good. There will always be online critics and haters, and you will never be able to please everyone. Since there are no rules on social media, much of the comments and online bullying will go unregulated.

FAKE NEWS

In a world where anyone and everyone feels entitled to share whatever they please, there is a staggering increase in misleading information available online. As an influencer, this directly affects you. First, it is critical that you thoroughly vet the brand you are promoting prior to any collaboration. It is also your responsibility to vet the products or services requested of you. It is imperative that you trust the source of your information, because the last thing you want to do as an influencer is to provide misleading or faulty information to your audience. One simple way to show transparency to your audience is to include the hashtag "#ad" when you're being paid to promote a product. This shows that there is a paid partnership between the influencer and the product. This way, the audience is aware of the partnership and can take the information with a grain of salt.

CLICKBAIT

Then there's the issue of clickbait. Clickbait is a form of false advertising. The goal of clickbait is to get users to click on pop-ups or ads. However, many internet marketers and influencers are starting to use clickbait tactics to lure in audiences under false pretenses. This will only cause you to lose potential or current audience members, though, as they can no longer trust you. The moment you inundate a user with clickbait, you've lost them.

HARASSMENT AND BULLYING

While there will always be bullies, online trolls, and those with a generally negative attitude, as an influencer you will unfortunately likely encounter these types of people online, even within your niche or inner circle. Social media breeds feelings of jealousy, comparison, and greed. If you've decided to become an influencer, you must have a strong will, thick skin, and some sense of emotional maturity. Staying above the negativity and hate will be the only way to succeed as an influencer, both personally and professionally. Stay focused on you. As an influencer, you have thousands of eyes on you, watching every move you make and every word you say. Those who foster hate, unhealthy comparison, jealousy, and generally negative attitudes are eventually seen by their audience and by brands. They are ultimately labeled as hard to work with or not the right fit.

AN INFLUENCER'S PERSPECTIVE ON THE NEGATIVE EFFECTS OF SOCIAL MEDIA

Morgan Haley (@findingmorgantyler)

"Every choice you make is scrutinized by thousands of people. It's a bit crippling at times. I've had death threats made, hate-mail sent, and even had people spy on me at local restaurants and gyms, only to report my every move to troll accounts. It used to make me want to never post again. But over the years I've learned you can only feel sad for those people and the lives they must lead that have led them to target so much hate toward someone they don't even know."

Tip: the internet is vastly different from the real world in that, from an influencer perspective, we are not able to choose our audience or those we interact with. When first starting out, try to keep an open mind, both in the brands and accounts you choose to follow and interact with.

ETHICS

This is a hot topic among psychiatrists, teachers, parents, and businesses alike. What are your social responsibilities as a brand and as an influencer? As a brand, are you responsible for actions taken by an influencer who represents you? As an influencer, should you be ethically driven to look into the brands you represent? These are questions that we do not have answers to. Currently, the research has not caught up with the trends, and we do not know the long-term effects of these situations.

A good example of the ethics of social-media influencers is the Fyre Festival, a fraudulent music festival that rose to fame by promotions from influencers and ultimately ended with jail time for the creators and a lawsuit filed against the influencers for misrepresentation of the service/product they were advertising. Who should be responsible for the impact of this huge catastrophe? Is it the responsibility of the customer to look into what they are buying? Is it solely up to the brand to be transparent? Is it the responsibility of the influencer to accurately represent what they are selling and disclose paid promotions? Should there be stronger government control, specifically from the FTC and other regulating bodies? These are all questions that we as a society need to be asking. We need to be learning and growing, while still protecting people from what could potentially be a problem.

While we await the research, there are some things that both brands and influencers can do now to help protect their decisions.

1. Both brands and influencers can do their due diligence by researching who they will be working with. Check on the collaborations and people with whom you align yourself and ensure that you are on the same page. It is up to you to look into the legitimacy and ethics of the companies you are promoting.

2. Be authentic! Tag your posts and be honest when you are sponsoring someone or are being sponsored. If you have nothing to hide, then hide nothing. This way, your audience and customers will always know what your

intentions are. Plus, it will add legal backing if you tag posts properly.

3. Know what data you are collecting and sharing. This ties into knowing and researching the companies with whom you partner. It is part of your responsibility to protect your followers and customers. Make sure that the proper precautions are put in place to protect everyone's data.

AVOIDING PR PROBLEMS

While receiving PR can be one of the most exciting new steps for growing influencers, you may soon discover that PR can sometimes lead to a multitude of problems. PR should take into consideration many of the same factors as accepting a sponsored collaboration (chapter 7), in that you should ensure the product is aligned with your account or beliefs. Don't just accept all PR because it's free.

Further, make sure you understand what it is you are agreeing to. If you are receiving product in exchange for posting, you are technically in an unpaid sponsored collaboration. However, if no contract was signed, you legally do not need to post once you have received the product, although you should be mindful of your reputation when making this decision.

PR can also become a problem when a brand starts to harass you after they have sent you something. They may send constant follow-up messages asking or suggesting you post. Remember though, if you have not agreed to posting and have not signed a contract saying you will post, you do not have to post anything you have received as a gift. You can help to mitigate this issue by kindly and respectfully contacting the brand, thanking them for the *gift*, and letting them know that if the circumstances feel right in the future you *might* post about the product, but at this time have no intentions of doing so. That should get your message across.

FOR BRANDS

Any brand that offers PR knows the drama that can arise from PR lists. Practically everyone wants to be on as many PR lists as possible. Not only can that create drama within a community, but it can also put an incredible amount of strain on the brand's PR or social manager. Often, influencers will see their friends or competitors on PR lists and wonder why they are not on the list as well. Sadly, this can lead to hostility, brand backlash, negative brand press, etc. While unfortunate, this inevitably weeds out influencers your brand would not want to partner with anyway.

Ultimately, it is *your* brand. You have complete autonomy over who you choose to collaborate with, whether it's via PR or some other channel. Choosing influencers for any type of collaboration should follow the guidelines set forth in chapter 7.

Brands can minimize issues surrounding PR by following these steps:

- Never lie to influencers—don't say your PR list is full unless it truly is. If you don't want to engage with a certain influencer who has contacted you for PR, tell them. Simply thank them for reaching out and let them know that at this time you don't believe a collaboration would be a good fit.

- Don't discriminate—this should be obvious, but it is stated because it's highly important.

- Remember to research influencers on your own—as discussed in chapter 7, it is important to do your own personal research on influencers with whom you wish to collaborate. While you can gain opinions and insights from others, it's important to be careful of others who may try to block influencers from others' lists.

- Don't harass influencers with emails or messages after you have gifted them a product—if they want to post they will. Harassing them will only turn them off from sharing your product.

- Be confident in your PR list/strategy—you can have whatever list or strategy you desire, and you don't owe influencers an explanation of it.

SUMMARY

As difficult as becoming an influencer can be, growing as an influencer is an even greater challenge. In fact, being an influencer can be quite demanding and time consuming due to the fake news, clickbait, and online bullying they regularly encounter. Despite all this, the key is to remain as authentic as possible. Tag your posts and be honest when you are sponsoring someone, or are being sponsored. Your audience will appreciate this, and it's actually what will enable you to grow in followers.

It's important for both brands and influencers to do their due diligence by researching who they will potentially be working with. Once an influencer is discovered by brands, this can be an exciting yet overwhelming time. Influencers will need to make sure of exactly what they are agreeing to and that they are protected.

As far as brands are concerned, they should follow these guidelines when it comes to PR:

- Never lie to influencers.
- Don't discriminate.
- Thoroughly research influencers and just don't take others' word.

- Don't harass influencers.
- Be confident in your PR list/strategy.

INFLUENCER SPOTLIGHT

SEATTLE GENTS

Instagram: @seattlegents

Seattle Gents is a collective of social-media influencers who have a passion for fashion, lifestyle, dining, travel, and hospitality. The members consist of individuals repre-senting several different styles, such as professional, street-wear, lifestyle, and casual fashion. They aim to influence the Seattle community and help others become inspired by men's fashion.

Q: Do you reach out to brands or wait for them to come to you?

A: Through my own fashion influencer page, I do not reach out to brands like I used to. When I first started, I would reach out to several brands to work with. Now that my page is going in a different direction, I'm not focusing on finding brand collabs. I'm focusing much of my time and effort on finding business for Seattle Gents, which is a collective of influencers. I spend a lot of time reaching out to brands to work with Seattle Gents.

Q: Tell a story about a brand collaboration that went really well.

A: One notable collaboration was with Rodd & Gunn. R&G is a New Zealand-based menswear company, and they opened their first store in Washington State earlier this year. I met the CEO a couple years back at a trade show in Vegas. Probably a year later, I hit him up and tried flagging him down. He referred me to a couple other people on his team, and after talking with someone for over a year we finally landed a collaboration! We helped them host a store opening event at Bellevue Square, and it was very successful. We invited our community out to check out their new store. Our network of influencers came to the event and hosted a small styling demonstration. It was interactive; the audience got involved and loved the styles they chose.

Q: How have you experienced community with other influencers?

A: Seattle Gents was founded on the basis of bringing together a community. I saw that there was a lack of a male-influencer community in Seattle, so I had a goal to build one. We started putting together meet-ups over two common interests: fashion and lifestyle. It rapidly grew, and we saw so much amazing collaboration with influencers come out of it. Brands wanted to work with us so that we could help spread the word and create content. My experience with community has been incredible. It brings people together, strengthens each individual brand, and allows us to make connections.

This complete interview is available in Appendix E on page 197.

11. THE FUTURE OF INFLUENCER MARKETING

WHERE IS THIS GOING?

Social media is rapidly changing, and Influencer Marketing must adapt to keep up. Micro-influencers, in-house influencers, and CGI influencers are three subgroups that are growing in popularity. Micro-influencers are attractive to brands because, although their audience is smaller, their engagement tends to be much more far-reaching. Because they haven't reached large-influencer status, they are still quite affordable, while remaining authentic to their followers.

Another current trend is that companies are now beginning to create and manage their own in-house influencer teams. This allows brands to have direct leadership and control over influencer campaigns. This, of course, can create issues with authenticity. Consumers tend to see through these in-house influencers early on, so the trend of the in-house influencer might be short-lived.

CGI, or computer-generated imagery, is another trend in Influencer Marketing that has begun to take off. Currently, Lil

Miquela, Bermuda, and Shudu are all CGI influencers. They have inspired others interested in 3D art to explore this area. Though this is a fad of sorts, it can provide the opportunity for greater ROI if a brand can leverage the public's interest.

With an increase in collaborations and cross-promotions, Influencer Marketing has become more about the collective rather than the individual. For example, there may be a few influencers that a brand consistently works with, and they may even network and collaborate as a team from time to time. This is happening more frequently, as the lines between niches become blurred. For example, a brand may want to work with influencers in the hair, makeup, and nail niches for an overall beauty campaign. As a result, these influencers can then cross-promote to each other's audiences.

While marketing used to be a long-term strategy, our plans now need to frequently pivot and adapt. This challenge is also what makes social media and Influencer Marketing so exciting. Opportunity abounds in uncertainty and change. Though investment is required, smart marketers look for the kinds of opportunities others miss to get ahead of the competition.

HOW CAN I PROTECT MYSELF FROM LOSING MY INVESTMENTS?

Life provides few guarantees. Business is no different. There is no foolproof strategy for protecting one's investments. However, a smart brand or influencer will do what they can to ensure their investments are as protected as possible. One of the challenges with Influencer Marketing is the speed at which the landscape is changing. Though new networks are not popping up as often as they did in the late 2000s, when social media was still sorting out which platforms would become dominant, changes are still happening practically every day. Many of these changes have the potential to provide huge opportunities—or to waste your time and money. Just as with any investment strategy, hedging and diversification are important forms of protection. If you rely entirely on a single platform, you stand to lose everything you've built if that platform falls out of favor or disappears completely.

However, even more pressing are the changing algorithms that determine if your content is going to be seen by your audience. These are important to watch closely and regularly. Stay on top of any changes and always be checking your metrics to make sure your engagement is not dropping as you grow. You can compare your own metrics to industry standards, or consult with other influencers or brands that are working in it every day. If you are seeing your engagement drop, it could be because you are producing less engaging content, or it could be that the platform changed its algorithm and is now showing your content to fewer followers.

On the other hand, these changes provide the opportunity to maximize growth and get ahead of your competition. If you stay on top of the changes better than those with whom you compete, you have the opportunity to take advantage and get a jump on your competitors. Keep your eye out for the next big network or other changes that you can use to your advantage to grow and achieve your goals. You can attend trade events, network with others in your field, or even host focus groups of young people to talk about what they're interested in and where they are spending their time. If you can find a way to be early on a new network, you have a much better chance of growing quickly.

SUMMARY

Smart brands and influencers will aim to ensure their investments are as protected as possible. The social-media landscape and algorithms are constantly changing, and there's no guarantee that you won't lose all that you've worked so hard for if a platform suddenly disappears.

On the other hand, these changes provide the opportunity to maximize growth. If you adapt to these changes more effectively than those with whom you compete, then you will be able to get a jump on your competitors.

INFLUENCER SPOTLIGHT

MOOREA SEAL

Instagram: @mooreaseal

Moorea Seal is the author of 52 Lists for Happiness, The 52 Lists Project, Make Yourself at Home, and founder of mooreaseal.com.

Q: Do you hire influencers for anything now?

A: Now I don't do a ton of hiring influencers for stuff. I have quite a variety of ways that, as a retailer, I've worked with influencers over the years. It started as an organic relationship that I had with other influencers, and I still have because I genuinely care about them. The people who actually care and build real relationships are the people that win.

In the early days of blogging and before we had a name for ourselves, we were just doing it because we were creative and wanted to be bigger than the whole narrative of being a boss girl. I honestly didn't resonate with the Sophia Amoroso narrative of being a girl boss because I thought it was pretty belittling and simplistic. It's no joke to be in business. As someone who built a little business on Etsy, I knew just how hard it was to build a brand and a business without having a degree in business. And, I had seen over the years the sort of manipulation that has been placed on women especially aspiring to be business owners and aspiring to be influencers. There's been a whole development of networking to that demographic.

There's a documentary on a company that shows that the world of influencers and blogging has become a world of massive pyramid schemes. They tell women that they want to empower them, that they believe in their voice. They get them to join their community to sell their stuff. I've seen huge pyramid schemes within essential oils and stay-at-home moms who are wanting to have a career as an influencer or trying to find a way to build out their own income. And many smart people in business are always looking for ways to do that. I mean, they're trying to maximize profit, and this is just one more way to do it. Now we have essential-oil parties. We have retail brands that sell clothing, and we have parties that could win you a car if you sell it in your home to your friends. That's all still happening within the influencer world, the Instagram world, the blogging world.

They're capitalizing on people's vulnerability. And that is what I fight the hardest against. I want to use my influence for good and for protecting and empowering people, because most of the people who are influencers are women. The first influencers were mostly women. Most of them were women who worked from home or who stayed at home, who had free time.

I have a lot of friends within the Mormon community who are women who I met through blogging in the early 2000s because they weren't allowed by their family, their culture, their religion to be working mothers. But their way around it was to start a blog and to build a side hustle through that. It's a really interesting and beautiful story of empowerment and women trying to find their voice, and women trying to have ownership of their own lives.

Q: Talk to me about how you're trying to make the world of influencers a more positive place for people.

A: What I've learned from doing influencer work and being a retailer over the last ten years is that above all else, I want to be an advocate, and I want to be someone who fights for people's personal wellness, which has also become an incredibly hot topic because of social media and influencers. Kids are growing up in such a different world when it comes to interacting with social media than I did. We got cell phones at the end of high school. We got Facebook our freshman year of college, when it was only accessible to college students. I was a part of the first generation of so many of these different things.

I have two younger sisters, one is nine years younger than me, and I'm observing her life that is under the influence of influencers and the sorts of pressures and expectations that everyday people now have to create a brand for themselves. With the pressure of influencers, people now feel like they must create an Instagram for their baby so that they have that lineage for when they get to when they're twenty and they want to start their own brand. We're in a crazy culture of this narrative where being an influencer is core to being a human almost. Having your brand, having your color palette, having your typography. Everything that I studied, it's fascinating to now see young people, twelve-year-olds, thirteen-year-olds hopping on Instagram and deciding that they have to create who they are, who they must present to the world so they can get deals and get free stuff, so they can build their own business someday.

This complete interview is available in Appendix E on page 210.

12. CONCLUSION

NOW THAT YOU UNDERSTAND WHAT INFLUENCER MARKETING IS all about, the question you need to ask yourself is if it is right for you. Consider your motivations. Do they fit within the opportunities provided by social media? Of course, the first step is always the hardest, but you will know early on if it's something you want to continue with long-term. Start by defining your goals, then work backwards. Then you can make small steps every day toward achieving those goals.

There is no doubt that launching a new project is tough, especially when it's something you've never done before. Chances are, however, at some point in your life you've already been here. You might have taken a job you didn't feel quite qualified for, or begun a project you knew little to nothing about, but you took the chance to learn something new. Entering the world of Influencer Marketing is no different. It's an acquired skill set, and as of now there aren't a lot of hard rules to follow. You can choose to be any kind of influencer you want to be, and brands can run any type of campaign they wish. Being successful in the Influencer Marketing space is subjective and entirely dependent on personal drive, creativity, ambition, and desire to succeed.

In closing, and if you remember nothing else from this book, keep these three key messages in mind:

1. *Don't worry too much about following the "rules."* When it comes to account creation, campaign design, and measurement strategies, the possibilities are endless. Just be sure to remain ethical when it comes to your audience, contractual obligations, and FTC compliance. Only you will know what is best for your account and brand, and you should never avoid taking risks or trying something new, stepping outside the box, or creating something from scratch.

2. *Be unique.* It's an over-saturated world for both influencers and brands. Utilize your creativity to overcome this. Even within your niche, you should be able to find something that makes you stand out, whether it is a new type of campaign, influencer affiliate program, or a quirk about you that you can incorporate into your account. Again, the possibilities are endless.

3. *Focus on your audience.* It's easy to get caught up in everything else happening around you—for example, your blogger friend's latest collaboration or your niche competitor. If you only focus on outperforming those around you, you will inevitably only be as successful as they are. From a brand standpoint, it will be important to measure the success of competitors, as it will give you insight into what works well and what doesn't without having to experience those trials and tribulations for yourself. Simply focus on how you can do better and let go of whatever is outside your control.

Influencer Marketing isn't going away anytime soon. In fact, it's only gaining momentum. Now's the time to get in on the action, if you feel the urge. Use this book as a guide as you get started, and even as you begin collaborating with brands. The social-media world is waiting for you. Who you are tomorrow begins with what you do today![16]

INFLUENCER SPOTLIGHT: ABOUT THE AUTHOR,
JUSTIN BLANEY

Instagram: @justinblaney

About Justin

Justin Blaney, D.M. is the number-one bestselling author of fifteen books. He also publishes an app that features his writing, which can be found at www.justinblaney.com/ app. Justin has been using, writing, and speaking about social media since 2006 and is followed by more than one million people.

Q: How did you get started in social networking?

A: My first social network was Myspace. I remember pimping my profile back in 2006 when I was getting into writing music and found it to be a great way to share my work. Facebook was just coming on the scene. It seemed so shockingly simple, with its white and blue colors and little ability to modify one's page. A lot of social networks were forming at the time and no one really knew which would take off. So I created accounts with most of them, claiming my name whenever possible. Eventually, I transitioned from music to writing and began to find an audience on my Facebook page, which grew faster as I found my voice and grew in my authenticity—something that didn't come naturally to me. I can't say that I've ever been truly comfortable or

---

16   Tim Fargo, developgoodhabits.com.

in my element on social media. I don't love sharing my life with the public, but I do love the ability to reach new and old readers, to listen to them and share our lives together in some small way. Social media has hovered for me somewhere between a chore and a magical way to reach so many that I likely never would have if I'd been born twenty years earlier. Overall though, I am thankful I have had the opportunity to use these tools and technology to connect with so many. I really can't imagine my life without it.

Q: If Instagram/YouTube were to be permanently deleted, what would you do?

A: One of the reasons I've invested heavily in building my own app is to protect myself against the possibility of my audience disappearing due to changing algorithms or even the closing of a social network I rely upon. I worked for years to build a following of over one million people on my Facebook page, only to see the number of impressions per post dwindle from 70 percent of my followers to less than 1 percent. I could pay to boost my posts and show them to those followers, but I don't have a business model to profit from my Facebook posts that would provide enough income to offset the costs of promoting the posts. So I have pretty much written off Facebook and the page I invested the most in for years. I switched to Instagram as my main page, but they too have been reducing the number of followers who see my posts organically from about 70 percent to now less than 10 percent in many cases. All that to say, I've been preparing for the loss of my audience now that this has happened to me twice, and investing in other forms of communication with my followers. Though this is expensive, time consuming, and difficult, I feel strongly that this is what is necessary to continue to reach the audience I've worked so hard to build.

Q: Have you ever experienced the negative side-effects of social media?

A: The bigger you get, the more hate you get. This is a simple fact of life. I had a very hard time with the negativity and hate on the internet when I was starting out. I'll always remember the first one-star review I received on a book I'd worked five years on. I was crushed. How could someone take time out of their day to trash my most prized work, and make hurtful and very personal insults to me, a person they know nothing about? These questions have been asked by many on the receiving end of these forms of negativity. I received some advice at the time. I was told to consider hateful comments as compliments. It means someone is thinking about me and taking time to write about their thoughts on the internet. That means my content is out there and causing reactions. I'd rather have that than nothing. At the time, this advice didn't resonate with me. I just wanted people to be nice. Unfortunately, that's not the case and it probably won't be any time soon. So eventually I did learn to let these insults roll off me, and frankly I don't care anymore what people say about my work or me for that matter. This is really the only option if one is going to put themselves out into the public eye for criticism and not be depressed all the time when people aren't kind.

Q: What is the number-one tip or piece of advice you would give to an influencer starting out?

A: Don't try to be an influencer. I'd recommend that you just do what you want, and do it as well as you can. Don't go into it with preconceived notions, and you won't be disappointed. If you want to have a chance at making it big, you're going to have to do a lot of learning and growing. You're going to have to do what I call checking all the boxes. That means you figure out all of the best things that one can do, and then you do every single one of them. I've seen people grow from nothing to 100,000 followers or more in less than a year. I know it can be done, but it's usually because these people checked all the boxes and they had luck on their side. I just think setting out with this as your primary goal is a recipe for disappointment and frustration. Do social media because you love it. Share what you want. Make it a part of your life if that makes you happy. If you do all this and end up making money and being famous, great. If not, you won't be disappointed and you'll be happy for doing all the things you wanted to do.

INFLUENCER SPOTLIGHT: ABOUT THE AUTHOR,

KATE FLEMING

Instagram: @the.skincare.diary, a skincare and lifestyle blog

About Kate

I wanted to share a bit about my journey, where I came from, and how I got into Influencer Marketing, which eventually led to this book. I'd also like to share some commonly asked questions about my journey and influencing.

My story, like most, began long before I ever made an Instagram account. I've been a gymnast, a server, a baker, a college dropout—all of which led to my current position as an analytics engineer.

In 2013, I made the bittersweet decision to drop out of college after only my first semester. I was young, working full-time at a local bakery, and had stumbled upon a tech startup that I began interning at a few months prior. I didn't know it at the time, but dropping out of college would become the best decision I had ever made, both for myself and my career. Life was busy, full, and in the naivety of my 18-year-old mind I was too busy to be bothered with classes on books I'd already read, or lectures on concepts I felt I'd learned in middle school. I was ready for the real world. I was ready for something real. After dropping out, I was eager to round out my jaded, self-taught coding and technical skill set. I applied for placement at a local trade school. Months of excruciatingly long eighty-hour workweeks passed—absorbing information, and putting to test various concepts learned hours prior. There were days spent sleeping in a cool, dark, basement classroom. It wasn't glamorous, but it paid off when I was named youngest graduate ever and had three job offers.

My days now are spent analyzing data, writing code, and poking around the web. In my free time you'll find me in the air pursuing my pilot's license and running the Skincare Diary. Given my background, I don't sound much like an influencer based on common stereotypes, but I can promise you, over the past year, I have lived and breathed every moment of it.

Q: Did you want to become an influencer?

A: The short answer: no. I never had the desire to become an influencer, and I never thought in my entire life that I would be considered one. I still don't particularly identify with the term and think of myself more as a content creator. I began my influencer career unknowingly when my passion for skincare and technology fatefully collided. Out of boredom, I had set out to teach myself Squarespace development. Only moments in, I realized my fake website would need a name. In about two minutes, I came up with The Skincare Diary from my passion for skincare, and I continued on with development. It was months later that I thought it might be fun to share some of the research and reviews I had done on various aspects of skin and skincare. So I created an Instagram account and began posting. Much to my surprise, it caught some traction and continued to grow.

Q: What is the most difficult part of being an influencer?

A: As someone who didn't necessarily want this life, the hardest part is the separation between real life and online life, both from a time-management and mental perspective. It's easy to get caught up in everything happening online. In real life, you pick your friends and you pick your circle. Online, you're not given that luxury. You're exposed to things you wouldn't normally see or hear in real life, and you don't have much of a say over any of it. I think it's incredibly important to maintain a healthy real life and have something substantial to fall back on at the end of every day. Social media, most often, is not real life. Aside from that, the other difficulty has been managing time. Between a real job and real life, it can get messy trying to keep up with it all.

Q: What advice would you give to someone wanting to become an influencer?

A: Anyone can do it; you just have to go for it. When starting out, you're going to be bombarded by a culture you didn't know existed. Regardless of how much time you've spent on social media before, it will be a complete eye opener. When starting out, it's important to remain agnostic, both of brands and other people. A lot of the time I see new influencers coming into a space and immediately being drawn into cliques or a religious-like worship of larger accounts. This will limit you in the long run, not only professionally, but also in the way you think and operate your account. Lastly, don't become an influencer to start drama or become a cyber bully, and don't let the fame of being an influencer go to your head. You will never have enough followers to excuse unkind behavior.

Q: What advice would you give to brands?

A: Influencers are entire people outside of social media. We're tech workers, lawyers, athletes, servers, doctors—and we're smart. So often I see brands approach influencers as if they're children on a playground, unable to comprehend anything. There have been too many times I've felt a brand has tried to take advantage of my intellect by trying to slip things by me. Whether it's verbiage in a contract, or deliverable requirements as an example, throwing me into the stereotype of what it's perceived to be as an influencer.

Q: Signing Off

A: You should have a solid foundation upon which to build your account or your Influencer Marketing strategy. Whether you're a brand just getting into Influencer Marketing or someone who wants to become an influencer, remember, there have been those who came before you and there will be those in the next generation. It can be you; you just have to take the first step. Create, inspire, and be kind.

13. APPENDICES

APPENDIX A: SAMPLE SIMPLE CONTRACT WITH CONTENT GUIDELINES

Independent Contractor Agreement

Scope of Services: *Description of services to be provided.*

Details: *Details of the engagement or link to a content brief. This clause should include who is responsible for fulfilling the items or services necessary to complete the services listed within the scope.*

Who: *[influencer name]/@[socialhandle]*

When: *Date of campaign, content approval date, and content go-live date.*

Compensation: *Total payment, payment date, and method of payment. This clause should include fees for late payments and content reshoots.*

Rights: *A brand's rights to the content provided.*

Exclusivity: *Anything relating to non-compete information, e.g. brands or services to avoid during the duration of the campaign, if applicable*

Confidentiality: *A clause stating what information can be shared externally, during and after the campaign or collaboration.*

Expenses: *A clause stating all incurred fees during the term of the collaboration. Ex: necessary purchases to complete the scope of services such as travel, purchases, etc.*

Miscellaneous: *A clause outlining any terms not included in the sections above. It should detail what is to happen in the event of early contract termination, if the content or services in the scope must be redone, etc.*

Scope of Services

Post 1—[Product or service] [Content Approval Date] [Posting Date]

—Photo: [product or service]

—Caption: [guidelines]

—Caption tag guidelines: (any applicable @ or # mentions)

—Caption keyword requirements: clean/effective/sustainable/transparent

—Sponsorship disclosure: (#ad or #sponsored, if applicable)

—Any other subsequent content to be delivered in the first deliverable

Post 2—[Product or service] [Content Approval Date] [Posting Date]

—Photo: [product or service]

—Caption: [guidelines]

—Caption tag guidelines: (any applicable @ or # mentions)

—Caption keyword requirements: clean/effective/sustainable/transparent

—Sponsorship disclosure: (#ad or #sponsored, if applicable)

—Any other subsequent content to be delivered in the second deliverable

Signed _____

Date _____

Influencer/Content Creator

Signed _____

Date _____

APPENDIX B
EXAMPLE MARKETING PLAN FOR SEND IT RECORDS

Created by Marshall Kinzer, Max Boomer, and Guy Schoonmaker

Executive Summary

Seattle does not have high quality music studios that produce records quickly. Send It Records is the product of the founders' twenty-plus years of music-production experience and strives to help up-and-coming musicians make music better, faster, and at a lower price.

Company Overview

Send It Records is a new, creative music studio and recording company based out of Seattle, Washington. The company was founded by Marshall Kinzer and Evan Koessler as a Washington registered LLC. The business operates a studio in Ballard and two satellite studios in the Seattle area. Send It Records is always on the technological frontier of sound engineering so they can make music faster for their customers, while not lowering the quality of the music. At Send It Records we believe that every musician deserves to make commercial-quality music without spending their life savings. We know that the technological advances in production and recording allow us to make music faster than studios of the past. Artists should not have to spend the better part of a year trying to record an album. Send It Records is here to change the amount of time and money it takes to produce, mix, and master music. We are going to change the way music is recorded.

Industry Analysis

CURRENT STATE

The recording-studio industry is poorly represented locally. With 80 percent of recording studios being opened in Seattle before 2005, and with the Seattle area growing faster than anywhere over the last decade, the city is desperate for a new, modern studio. The market is currently controlled by seven high-end studios. These companies control all the corporate and commercial recording deals, adding up to 75 percent of the recording revenue in Seattle. The other 25 percent is a mix of home studios and smaller studios in the local area.

PROBLEMS

1. Music production and post-production on the West Coast is overpriced, not commercial-quality, or unreasonably time consuming.
2. Artists, singers, and rappers lack the technical expertise to produce their own instrumental music at a commercial level.
3. Seattle recording studios have expensive hourly rates and expensive costs of sound engineers.
4. Most Seattle recording studios do not offer the same person or team to partner with an artist's writing, production, mixing, and mastering.

SOLUTIONS

1. Our team of talented music producers provides speed and convenience for musicians in need of online or in-studio music production, mixing, and mastering.

2. We differentiate our service by offering music production that is better, faster, and less expensive than other studios, because we are more knowledgeable about new sound-engineering technologies.

3. We focus on developing relationships and partnerships with upcoming artists to best build their image and crystallize their vision. We do this by offering a professional, collaborative, and fun environment to make music.

4. Our pricing is by the song and not an hourly rate, so customers know that we are not focused on time, we are only focused on the product.

Client Testimonials

"You made me feel so comfortable recording! I cannot wait to finish my album with you."—WYATT ROOD

"I really like how your studio makes a song with me from start to finish. I have never been in a more collaborative music studio." —ALEXIS BROOKE

Products and Services

Send It Records is a Seattle-based recording company for established and up-and-coming artists. The company is a one-stop shop for songwriting, production, and post-production music services. This approach is appealing to online and local artists because it is either expensive or challenging for an artist to do it themselves. Artists recognize that Send It Records works hard to bring an artist's vision to life by partnering with them in the writing, recording, production and post-production processes.

Management

The partners at Send It Inc. are the perfect balance of creative genius and savvy business sense. Marshall Kinzer, our CEO, is finishing his EMBA from the University of Washington. He has a background in finance and working on Wall St. Evan Koessler, COO and head of production, is a classically trained pianist and an award-winning musician who has worked with major record labels. Evan has produced, mixed, and mastered for some of the biggest names in music. Together we have come up with a multi-faceted business that offers more value than our competitors by targeting an unsatisfied market.

Objectives

- Become the premier Seattle recording studio within two years
- Complete production and/or post-production for 120 songs in year one
- Generate $100,000 in revenue in year one
- Open a studio in a Los Angeles in 2020
- Open a studio in Portland in 2021

Mission

"We make music for people who need it."

Send It Records exists as a locally based recording studio whose mission is to partner with artists and musicians so that they can create industry ready release records. Send It Records' goal is to help talented musicians create music that they believe is the best expression of their artistic self. We want to make music that is better, faster, and cheaper than all other recording studios. We strive to help artists make music they are proud of by using new technologies and cutting-edge music software. The next two cities we plan to target, in 2020 and 2021, are Los Angeles and Portland. We will open studios in those cities by partnering with local engineers (we have many contacts in both cities), finding a location with them, building out acoustic treatment, and training the engineers for two weeks. In five years, it will be common knowledge that Send It Records has the top recording studios for quality and speed on the West Coast.

Branding and Social-Influencer Strategy Goals

1. Build brand identity
2. Brand awareness
3. Leads: Schedule ten business meetings from IG messenger over one month.

Audience Targeting

PLATFORM #1: INSTAGRAM

Jake Crocker (ongoing)
How we target: Direct messages and email.

Process of reaching out: Direct messages leading to coffee meet-up, leading to future collaborations.

What we offer: Audio services.

What we get: Awareness, leads, and larger audience.

Actions: Will tag Send It in posts and stories when he comes out to studio, and re-post music.

Illoquent (ongoing)
How we target: Direct messages and email.

Process of reaching out: Direct messages leading to coffee meet-up, leading to future collaborations.

What we offer: Audio services.

What we get: Awareness, leads, and larger audience.

Actions: Will tag Send It in posts and stories when he comes out to studio, and re-post music.

Alexis Brooke (ongoing)

How we target: Direct contact (already familiar).

Process of reaching out: Direct messages leading to coffee meet-up, leading to future collaborations.

What we offer: Full production work and posting of music.

What we get: Brand awareness, split on royalties, leads, re-posts.

PLATFORM #2: YOUTUBE—PARTNER WITH INFLUENCERS ON TUTORIALS

Sendai Mike (May 31)

How we target: Direct messages.

Process of reaching out: Direct messages leading to coffee meet-up, leading to future collaborations.

What we offer: Free promotion, awareness, content.

What we get: Audience building, brand awareness, leads, re-posts.

Altovisual (June)

How we target: Already contacted.

What we offer: Cinematic audio and scoring.

What we get: Website work, shared content, rebrand.

Johnny Darko (June)

How we target: Already contacted.

What we offer: Video of behind the scenes recording.

What we get: Website work, shared content, rebrand.

PLATFORM #3: LIVE EVENTS/SPACES

Justin's Event with Scarlett Parker (May 31)

How we target: Event already happened.

Process of reaching out: Will connect at event, get phone numbers, and reach out through Instagram with audience and follow up after event.

What we offer: Free live audio.

What we got: Five demos scheduled and four additional leads.

Nectar

How we target: Show up in person, try to schedule meeting, find mutual connection.

Process of reaching out: direct messages, showing up in person, connecting through existing

clients.

What we offer: Convenient recording location.

What we get: Will offer Nectar percentage of business that comes through venue.

Tractor Tavern

How we target: Connect through Bad Beaches. Back-up is show up in person, try to schedule meeting, find mutual connection.

Process of reaching out: Direct messages, showing up in person, connecting through existing clients.

What we offer: Convenient recording location

OTHER TARGETING/LIST BUILDING

- Curate list of potential local clients by reaching out to event spaces, offering percentage of business that is generated from contact lists that are shared.
- Culture Fest (music event, artists, and spoken word)

Our target audience is primarily musicians, singer-songwriters, producers, and rappers from the Pacific Northwest. We look for clients that are collaborative, creative, and have a passion for everything music. We want target partners that are professional, honest, and genuine.

Similar Influencers

1. Sendai Mike
2. Jake Crocker
3. Seattle Hip Hop
4. Illoquent

Competitors

1. Robert Lange
2. Studio X
3. Illoquent
4. ElectroKitty
5. Any Seattle recording studio or place of sound engineering

Influencer Partnering Strategy

Our strategy to target influencers as partners is driven by outreach and our company offerings. We plan to provide our services in exchange for being tagged and/or receiving mentions on Instagram. We will also use our relationships with partners to capture additional content for our own brand and Instagram stories.

Applying our strategy

1. We locate a potential partner via searching hashtags focused on music in the Pacific Northwest.
2. We message the potential partner with who we are and samples of our music.
3. We offer to have them come to our recording studio and meet in person.
4. We discuss what their needs are, and we look for an opportunity to help each other musically.
5. We provide free mixing, mastering, or a collaboration with the influencers.
6. We ask for photos and content.
7. We ask them to make a post tagging our studio.
8. We ask them to tag our studio in the project we worked on together.

Ideal influencers to partner with:

1. Sendai Mike
2. Jake Crocker
3. Seattle Hip Hop
4. Lil Mosey
5. Macklemore
6. Sam Lochow
7. Chris Adams

8. Monstercat

9. Illoquent

Advertising Plan

We plan to pay for ads once we get to 600 followers. We will be running Instagram, Facebook, Google, and YouTube ads. We plan to spend 4 percent of profits on advertising (based on previous revenues, approximately $400/month).

We also will be putting together an event every month for Send It Records. We plan to pay for this event with ticket sales, and we will staff the event by collaborating with artists and musicians. Our first event is Wednesday, June 5, for a Send It Records photo shoot. We have ten artists scheduled to come, including Scarlet Parke and Alexis Brooke.

Media Kit

We are scheduled for a photo shoot with almost all of our artists tomorrow. We are using this content for our Instagram, website, and artists pages. We plan to build our media kit using three photos of our studio, a photo of the founders, sample artist photos, and then stats for our engagement (depending on the audience). We will use our bio from the executive summary and our tag line of "Creating music with friends," or "Send It Records, the only studio in Seattle that does everything audio."

Statistics and Analytics

INSTAGRAM

We plan to use insights and statistical analysis of engagement to gauge whether it is driving our leads. We are currently tracking the sources of our leads and if they come from likes or comments. We have found a strong association and a P-score greater than .05

for comments, yet there does not seem to be a relationship with likes. We believe this is because people who are really interested in connecting take that extra step and comment.

We will use this data to decide our future plans for Instagram and how we will leverage it for new business and brand awareness.

YOUTUBE

We plan to use Google and YouTube analytics to learn which engineers are watching our tutorials and where they are from. We are looking to learn what content really connects with our future audience, and then we plan to replicate it. We will also be tracking leads that come from YouTube. We expect most to be mixing and mastering leads.

Events

We will track all attendees who are artists we have worked with, who we have a relationship with, and who are new. After an event, we can use this data to track what revenue came from a relationship because of the event and what percentage of the sale we attribute to the event. This will allow us to find an ROI (if we spent money) on generating business from an event we throw.

Mood and Branding

1. Bright and vibrant
2. Educational (Sound Engineering, Production, Mixing, and Mastering)
3. Includes photos, written information, and videos

Analytical Tools and Strategy

We plan to use the software program Planoly to schedule, organize, and track statistics of our Instagram efforts. As you can see below, we have chosen a daily posting strategy. We are going to take the first week to explore the best time to post in the morning for our followers. Below are the statistics for the first three days of our strategy.

Sample E-mail:

Hey "X Influencer,"

We are Send It Records, an up-and-coming recording studio in Ballard. Our studio focuses on working with local singer/songwriters, rappers, and artists, along with venues and other creators in the Seattle music scene who embody our studio's brand values of creativity, collaboration, and community. Our goal is to help artists make music they can be proud of. We offer a full suite of services to artists including recording, mixing, and song writing. We're continually looking to expand our brand in Seattle by partnering with people in the music and influencer communities who we think are a great representation of our studio and the brand identity we are working to cultivate. We have seen your content on "x, y, and z" platforms and think you would be a great partner to help grow our brand here in Seattle. [Insert tailored sentence including song names, social posts, other brand differentiators, etc.] We'd love the opportunity to discuss working with you on a social campaign or brand collaboration. Send us a note at this e-mail address if you are interested in talking with us further, or feel free to reach out to us via one of our social-media channels using the links below. Are you available to meet this week to discuss further opportunities? We would love to have you visit the studio and make some music.

Marshall Kinzer

CEO, Send It Records

Social links included in e-mail signature

Sample Instagram Direct Message (Influencer):

Hey "X Influencer,"

We really love your content! We think that your content would be a great fit for our brand at Send It Records. We are an up-and-coming recording studio in Ballard that focuses on recording, mixing, and songwriting. Our studio focuses on working with artists, venues, and other creators in the music space who embody the Seattle music scene and our studio's brand values. We'd love to discuss working with you on a social-media campaign or brand collaboration. Are you available to meet this week to discuss further opportunities? We would love to have you visit the studio and make some music.

Sample Instagram Direct Message (Venue):

Hey "X Influencer/Venue,"

We really love your content! We think that your venue and artist slate would be a great fit for our brand at Send It Records. We are an up-and-coming recording studio in Ballard that focuses on recording, mixing, and songwriting. Our studio focuses on working with artists, venues, and other creators in the music space who embody the Seattle music scene and our studio's brand values. We'd love to discuss working with you on a social-media campaign or brand collaboration. Are you available to meet this week to discuss further opportunities? We would love to have you visit the studio and make some music.

Sample Instagram Comment:

Hey "X Influencer!" We love your content! We'd love to discuss the opportunity to work together on an Instagram campaign or brand collaboration in the future! Shoot us a DM if you're interested.

APPENDIX C
GLOSSARY OF TERMS

Advertising plan: a promotion blueprint that, when followed, provides the direction for companies and businesses to bolster sales.

Algorithm: a set of parameters performed by a computer to output a function. Most commonly referred to when discussing Instagram, Facebook, and Google. Algorithms in the social space determine how content is seen by an audience and how it is promoted. They often dictate performance of the content.

Analytic tools and strategy: a blueprint to evaluate your marketing effectiveness. The strategy should include a plan to use analytic tools to measure effectiveness of the campaign.

Audience targeting: the process of targeting a specific consumer or demographic based on data to ensure marketing influencers are targeted in the right direction.

Bio: a social media bio refers to a short text snippet that explains who the user or account is and what it is for. All social platform accounts for both influencers and brands should utilize a comprehensive bio.

Brand outreach strategy: a strategy for the way that key messages are delivered to the target audience. A brand outreach strategy includes a number of methods by the influencer to ensure that brand is top of mind for the audience.

Branding and/or branding guidelines: a document that governs the look and feel elements of a brand. Brand guidelines often dictate how marketing collateral can be used.

Clickbait: a marketing strategy that evokes just enough curiosity from the reader via the article or headline to instigate engagement.

Often, clickbait articles provide factually incorrect or incomplete information.

Competitors: another company selling a similar product.

Content calendar: the process of creating a calendar to push various content to gain a competitive advantage in marketing.

Content types: video, picture, blog, etc.

Conversion Rate: a common metric measured within social media that relates to the percentage of people who completed an intended action. Examples include: swipe-ups to a blog post, downloads of a specific piece of content, etc.

Corporate structure: the various departments or business units that make up a company. Corporate structure is often dependent on the industry in which the company operates.

CTA (Call to Action): the desired next step the audience or readers should take. Ex: a "buy now" button at the top of a brand's webpage.

Current state analysis: a process by which a company documents current processes and procedures, typically with an eye on process improvement.

Differentiation factors: the process of creating special products that separate a business or organization from the competition.

Direct Message: private messages sent from audience members to a social account's inbox.

Engagement Rate: a common social metric used to measure the average engagement of an audience on a social page. It is calculated based on likes, comments, and total audience. (Refer to chapter 9 for the formula.)

Financing: the act of providing funding for marketing activities that will improve product position.

Goals: usually in Influencer Marketing, the goal is to promote user awareness of a product.

Hashtag (#): a tag used by social platforms to categorize content. Most social platforms allow users to find content by searching for specific hashtags, which in turn typically provides more reach to those accounts that utilize them.

Ideal influencers to partner with: the process of identifying which social-media platforms to partner with to promote products.

Impressions: the total number of times a piece of content is viewed.

Influencer partnering strategy: includes the ways in which you plan to use social media as a partner to promote your product.

Keywords: words used to optimize search ability of content across web and social-media platforms.

Media kit: the kit that influencers bring to companies or brands for collaboration. A media kit consists of ways in which an influencer can help push a brand.

Mood board: a type of collage consisting of visuals, text, and sample objects that can convey a certain mood or idea.

Pricing sheet: the price for hiring an influencer.

Profit plan: the plan to increase profits through an Influencer Marketing campaign. This is not always necessarily the goal.

Pro-formas: the methods by which companies or firms calculate financial results using certain presumptions.

APPENDIX D
TOOLS

For as many social platforms and options as influencers have to reach their audience, there are many more tools that have been created to help them be more efficient and effective in their work. This section describes a number of the most popular and helpful tools.

POSTING AND HASHTAG TOOLS:

1. Buffer is a software application for both mobile and web. Buffer is designed to manage accounts in social networks by providing the means for a user to schedule posts to Twitter, Facebook, Instagram, Instagram Stories, Pinterest, and LinkedIn, as well as analyze their results and engage with their community.
2. Hootsuite is a social-media management platform whose system's user interface takes the form of a dashboard, and supports social network integrations for Twitter, Facebook, Instagram, LinkedIn, Google+, and YouTube.
3. Display Purposes is an online tool designed to help you find the best hashtags for your Instagram profile to get more followers, likes, and reach. This simple web tool will suggest a list of the best tags to use based on any base hashtag you give it. Plus, it will cross out any negative or overused spam tags, and provide interesting relevant terms in its place.

WEBSITE CREATION TOOLS:

1. Wordpress.org—A platform that allows for any type of customization. Be careful to not confuse this for wordpress.

com, which is a host, similar to Bluehost below. While you can use WordPress for hosting with a small monthly fee, you can also download the WordPress system for free and use it on any other host you wish to use. The free Word-Press is at the *.org* location.

2. Bluehost—A third party website-hosting provider, which allows for hosting changes related to traffic volume and other factors.

3. ThemeForest—A bountiful and inexpensive source for WordPress themes that you can install and modify yourself with zero to very little knowledge of programming.

4. iStock photo—A great source for video, illustrations, and images without resorting to stealing content from the internet (something ethical content creators never do).

5. Domains.google.com—a low-cost and easy-to-use domain registry service. Besides low-cost registry fees, you can use Google to establish free privacy, which means the public won't know the true owner of the domain. The domain you register on Google must be pointed at whatever host you select for the website to work properly. Tutorials and help documents on both your host and domain registrar can help you to accomplish this.

6. Upwork.com—A marketplace of freelancers who can help you with just about anything, from setting up your website to assisting you virtually. Prices per hour range from as little as four dollars to over one hundred dollars. You can find contractors around the world who fit your needs and expectations.

7. Fiverr.com—A freelancer marketplace much like Upwork, but on a lower scale. Freelancers on Fiverr sell five-dollar gigs, but don't let the price fool you. Most projects will likely cost much more than five dollars. However, if you're

looking for something quick and easy, Fiverr may be your best bet.

Below are Key Performance Indicator tracking tools mentioned elsewhere in the book:

KPI Tracking Tool	Price	Description
Google Analytics	Standard Version: Free Premier Version: $150K	Uses JavaScript to collect information about website, including site visits, etc.
Crazy Egg	$24 per month	Heat-mapping software that will tell you where the user spends their time on websites.
Followerwonk	$79 per month	Helps users dig deeper into their Twitter following to understand who their followers are.
Brandwatch	Pro Version: $1000 per month	A company in the UK that sells three products, including Consumer Research, Audiences, and Vizia. All of these products help companies monitor their social-media presence.
Mixpanel	Starts at $999 per year	Tracks user interactions with web and mobile applications. Provides tools for targeted communications with these applications.

BrandMentions	Starts at $49 per month	Monitors the number of times a brand is mentioned on the internet.
Sprout	Professional license: $149/month Advanced license: $249/month	Finds people who love your brand through social interactions.
Meltwater	Basic package $10–25/month Extensive apps $100/month	Software as a service that monitors brand performance compared to the competition.
Fohr	Does not provide public pricing	Membership network that connects brands with influencers.
TapInfluence	Does not provide public pricing	Provides three levels of Influencer Marketing software.
Agorapulse	Small company: $79/month Large company: $159/month Extra-large company: $239/month Enterprise: $399/month	Social-media management software that helps companies drive engagement and moderate social-media mentions.

Hootsuite	Professional: $29/month Team: $129/month Business: $599/month Enterprise: (custom pricing)	Social-media management platform.
Tailwind	$9.99/month (paid annually) $15/month.	Helps companies save time by optimizing the time for posts on Instagram and Pinterest.
NetBase	Basic: up to $200/month Extensive: $300–$1,000/ month	Social-media analytics company that helps businesses collect data from social media.
Keyhole	Professionals: $199/month Corporations: $599/month Agencies & Enterprises: $999/month	Tracks hashtags on Twitter, Instagram, and Facebook.

APPENDIX E
INFLUENCER SPOTLIGHTS

Portions of these spotlights appear throughout the book. The entire transcript is included in this appendix.

INFLUENCER SPOTLIGHT: KATY YATES

Maker, Sweet Littles Handmade

Instagram: @sweetlittleshandmade

Sweet Littles Handmade was founded in 2006 to fill a void in the children's stuffed-doll market. After struggling to find boy and gender-neutral dolls, we decided to make our own. Striving to create unique and very child friendly heirloom dolls for your babes, we create boy and girl dolls to meet all your snuggly needs.

Q: If Instagram/YouTube were to be permanently deleted, what would you do?

A: I would cry. There is so much of my life and memories wrapped up in those tiny squares. It seems so petty, but it was such a huge part of my life and helped mold me into who I am today. Part of my identity lives there.

Q: Have you ever experienced the negative side-effects of social media? (Bullying, trolls, etc.) How has this affected you?

A: So many copycats! And people who just don't realize that there is an actual human on the other side of the screen. I don't actively use my business page any longer. I recently did some work there and was immediately reminded of how thick-skinned you need to be.

Q: What is the number-one tip or piece of advice you would give to an influencer starting out?

A: Be authentic! If you want to grow and create a great following be yourself! There is this amazing opportunity to bring social change and insight into the world through social media! But if you aren't being you, everyone will see that.

Q: Number-one tip for brands looking to engage an influencer?

A: Know your customer! There is nothing more ridiculous than having a brand reach out that clearly hasn't even looked at your profile! When a brand reaches out that my following wouldn't connect with, it is a waste of my time and theirs, and none of us have time for that!

Q: How did you get started as an influencer?

A: I wouldn't call myself an influencer—I think it is a side effect of building community. It is a pretty special side effect! But my goal was never to gain influence, only to build community.

Q: Who do you like to work with and why?

A: My favorite is working with people and brands that are just starting! That's when I can see my influence the most! When I make a post and their business blows up, or if I can help pair them with an influencer who can do that for them, those are the people I want to surround myself with.

Q: How do you measure the effectiveness of your campaigns?

A: If you can't track your marketing then you are doing it wrong! There is a plethora of stats and data points that need to be followed. Everything from impressions, to clicks, to sales and referrals! If you are blindly marketing yourself, then you will not know when to pivot or reassess.

Q: How did you grow your platform?

A: My entire platform has grown via networking. First, I had to find out who my customer is. Then, I found like-minded companies and brands and reached out with the goal of mutual growth. From there, I continually aligned with brands that supported my vision and I theirs. Not only do I get to help others this way, but I am also growing a following that is my customer! So my sales grow too.

Q: Do you believe in advertising to gain followers?

Yes, I have paid to be in magazines and have articles written. I have provided my product for print work as well as to other influencers. I only do this when I can track the data, like in any marketing situation! I am also upfront about my expectations, whether it be a certain amount of photos or a deliverable.

Q: Where do you feel Influencer Marketing and influencers in general are going in the next two to three years?

A: If I am truly honest, I don't think that influencers have a long future. I think all things social media evolve very quickly, and as I watch technology grow and morph the need for influencers decreases. Will people still influence? Of course! But at the level we are using influencers now, not so much.

INFLUENCER SPOTLIGHT: SEATTLE GENTS

Instagram: @seattlegents

Seattle Gents is a collective of social-media influencers who have a passion for fashion, lifestyle, dining, travel, and hospitality. The members consist of individuals representing several different styles, such as professional, streetwear, lifestyle, and casual fashion. They aim to influence the Seattle community and help others become inspired by men's fashion.

Q: Do you reach out to brands or wait for them to come to you?

A: Through my own fashion influencer page, I do not reach out to brands like I used to. When I first started, I would reach out to several brands to work with. Now that my page is going in a different direction, I'm not focusing on finding brand collabs. I'm focusing the majority of my time and effort on finding business for Seattle Gents, which is a collective of influencers. I spend a lot of time reaching out to brands to work with Seattle Gents.

Q: Tell a story about a brand collaboration that went really well.

A: One really notable collaboration was with Rodd & Gunn. R&G is a New Zealand-based menswear company, and they opened their first store in Washington State earlier this year. I met the CEO a couple years back at a trade show in Vegas. Probably a year later, I hit him up and tried flagging him down. He referred me to a couple other people on his team, and after talking with someone for over a year, we finally landed a collaboration! We helped them host a store-opening event at Bellevue Square and it was very successful. We invited our community out to check out their new store. Our network of influencers came to the event and hosted a small styling demonstration. It was interactive, as the audience got involved and loved the styles they chose.

Q: How have you experienced community with other influencers?

A: Seattle Gents was founded on the basis of bringing together a community. I saw that there was a lack of a male-influencer community in Seattle, so I had a goal to build one. We started putting together meet-ups over two common interests: fashion and lifestyle. It rapidly grew, and we saw so much amazing collaboration with influencers come out of it. Brands wanted to work with us so that we could help spread the word and create content. My experience with community has been incredible. It brings people together, strengthens each individual brand, and allows us to make connections.

INFLUENCER SPOTLIGHT: BRENDA STEARNS

Content creator

Instagram: @she_plusfive

Brenda Stearns is a dedicated mother of five, home educator, social media influencer, and content creator. Brenda created @ she_plusfive to inspire women worldwide by sharing honest stories that make motherhood relatable, authentic, and beautiful. She has been featured by Aleteia, A Plus, Daily Mail, Daily Mail TV, Telemundo Lifestyle, Today's Parent magazine, UK magazine Take a Break, and Latin American publications such as Crecer, Boa Forma, and Ohlala.

Q: Do you want to be an influencer?

A: I believe we all are influencers in our own way. We all have a circle of people that we can influence, for good or bad. In the world of social media, I have been given the opportunity and honor to have a big audience. While that was never my initial goal, I guess in that sense, yes, I am an influencer.

Q: If Instagram/YouTube were to be permanently deleted, what would you do?

A: Go on with my life and move onto the next thing that God brings my way. I truly believe there are seasons in life for everything, and change can be a good thing.

Q: Have you ever experienced the negative side-effects of social media? (Bullying, trolls, etc.) How has this affected you?

A: Yes! Daily. At the beginning of my social-media journey, it would affect me a lot. I would focus on that negative comment, unconsciously letting it affect how I went about the rest of the day. I think now things have changed a bit. I've grown some thick skin. Comments don't hurt as much. Eighty percent of the time people genuinely care and think they're giving good advice by telling you how to live your life, etc. There's always that 20 percent who are plain just trying to poke at you. Just smile and move on. It's not worth your time or energy.

Q: How is this influencer movement negatively or positively affecting society?

A: What should influencers do to be a more positive influence? Influencers need to be more genuine about their collaborations. Taking into consideration your audience and their loyalty to your platform. Not just doing it for the money.

Q: What is your least favorite part about brand collaborations?

A: Brands demanding so much content for no pay.

Q: How do you feel about #ad posts?

A: Ads are everywhere! Magazines, radio, TV, Facebook, and all around us! When I see an influencer posting an ad, I feel proud of them. I know the amount of time it takes behind the scenes to create one piece of content. I know the work of emailing back and forth with brands and keeping your part of the contract. It's hard work! And a lot of people don't realize that.

Q: What is the number-one tip or piece of advice you would give to an influencer starting out?

A: Build a community of loyal followers, get to know them on a personal basis. Then focus on your content. What are you bringing to the table, and how is that benefiting your audience? Pitch to brands. Know your worth! Don't give up!

Q: Number-one tip for brands looking to engage an influencer?

A: Communication is key! I love it when a brand responds promptly to my questions, and they get bonus points if they pay my rate.

Q: How did you get started as an influencer?

A: It all kind of happened on its own. It wasn't my intention or goal, but once I saw the potential, I took an online course. I learned how to be a better content creator and how to build better relationships online.

Q: What are your ambitions for your career?

A: To keep being a source of inspiration for others and grow my audience. To branch out into YouTube and start my own family channel there as well. Our goal is to get sponsored travel and document our adventures.

Q: How much money do you earn? Where does the money come from? What do you see as opportunities to increase your earnings?

A: It varies depending on how many collaborations I get per month. Some months I have none and others I'll have three! I'd say average about $1,000 per month. I think I can definitely increase my rates and take on more collaborations to monetize my Instagram, so we are going to move in that direction soon.

Q: How do you think working with influencers is different than other forms of marketing?

A: Influencer Marketing works because influencers work hard in building real relationships with their audience. You won't get the same result from a magazine ad.

Q: What do you look for in brand partnerships?

A: The ethos of their brand has to align with my lifestyle. The goal for me is to have long-term relations with the brand.

Q: What are the most important aspects of your contracts with brands?

A: Their terms of the collaboration, deliverables being asked, compensation, when they're due for approval, and when payment is expected.

Q: Do you believe in advertising to gain followers?

A: I don't agree with artificially growing your audience. Whether it's bots, engagement groups on telegram, buying followers, follow/unfollow, and whatever else is out there now. I truly believe in quality over quantity. At the end of the day, it's not about the numbers but the relationships you're cultivating.

Q: What are your pet peeves about working with brands?

A: Not valuing our time and work as influencers. We are saving them a ton of money. They're not paying models, makeup, style, photographers; they don't have to rent a studio or do any sort of planning for the content. We do it all. Just please take that into consideration when reaching out to influencers.

INFLUENCER SPOTLIGHT: SARAH SIMON

Artist and Author, TheMintGardener

www.themintgardener.com

Instagram: @themintgardener

Sarah Simon is the designer, artist illustrator, and author at The-MintGardener. With a continually blooming following of botanical and art lovers alike, Sarah shares her teaching talents locally in Seattle, where she regularly instructs watercolor classes to students of all skill levels.

Q: Do you want to be an influencer?

A: Even hearing that name kind of makes me go uhhh—I'm not 100 percent sure, but that's probably just part of my personality.

My primary goal is to be an artist, but I looked it up and it defined social media influencer as a user on social media who has an established credibility in a specific industry.[17] So by that definition, I'd absolutely love that. I have an established credibility in the watercolor world, the artistic community, as well as the Instagram community. I am seen as authentic, and I am approached by a lot of brands that want me to use their product or show their product. A rule I like to follow is that I don't post about something unless I absolutely love it. If I love it, I would post about something even if I am not getting paid! In a way, I believe that helps me to be true to myself. I let people know when they reach out that if I am not a fan, and if it doesn't feel like a good fit for my audience, then I am not going to share about it. For example, Winsor & Newton is a fabulous brand of paint. They are hundreds of years old, from England. I have been using their paint as props in my stylings since the very beginning. They have never paid me, but they have just recently started sending me products and they are actually becoming sponsors for my book tour in 2020. On the national book tour, they have offered to create a custom set of color palettes that's going to be amazing, and basically every attendee that comes to my workshop will get this custom palette. Yes, I do want to be an influencer in a way that it establishes credibility, and I do have access to a large audience, and I do like to share with others because of the virtue of products that I believe are good for the art.

Q: If Instagram or YouTube were permanently deleted, what would you do?

A: I would keep painting! I painted before. I'll paint after. For me, painting and creating is a part of who I am. If I didn't paint, I'm not

---

17   Blake Stimac, "What Is a Social Media Influencer and How to Become One," Wix Blog, May 22, 2018, https://www.wix.com/blog/2018/05/social-media-influencer.

100 percent sure if I'd be able to express myself fully. There were many years when I didn't paint, and I'd just withdraw. I felt very frustrated. So I have learned that in order to be happy, I have to paint. Social media is a way to share that, to influence and inspire others, and to also be influenced and inspired by others. But if they were to disappear tomorrow, I'd still paint.

Q: Have you experienced negative side-effects of social media, and how has it affected you?

A: Yes, absolutely! I have experienced a decent amount of copying. I've experienced bullying, or people making comments that they don't think I'd read as a person. What I've learned to do with that kind of bullying is to shake it off. You realize that when people comment it's not really a reflection of you. When they say something nasty, it's not a reflection of me, or my work, or what I'm sharing. It's a reflection of how they are feeling. Sometimes it sickens me and makes me sad, but I just kind of like shake it off. I have a group of girls that I have actually met through Instagram. They are amazing painters and creative. We just kind of run those things by each other, like copying, copyright infringements, and then also bullying. It helps to have a community of people that are willing to talk and this kind of dispels the pain of a bullying comment. It also helps you laugh at it too. I usually end those conversations by laughing or feeling sad and hoping that people are OK.

Q: How is this influencer movement negatively or positively affecting society? What should influencers do to be a more positive influence?

A: That's an interesting question! My husband would say—he's a financial advisor, and so anti-Instagram—he thinks that it sucks time. I would say it is interesting in our society, and I don't think we can go backwards now that we have had this. The way we can connect with one another is like having a digital pen pal. Humans crave connection and the ability to relate, and Instagram and social media and YouTube—we can connect now with all of these things in a more engaging way than we have ever been able to do before. So I think it's positive, but I also believe that people will find what they look for. So I feel like if people are looking for negative things on social media, that's what they are going to find. They are going to focus on the negatives just like they focus on the negative things in life. Every day I choose to really try to anticipate and to enjoy. I believe that social media can be bad like anything, and can be used for bad, but I choose to look for the good. If you choose to interact with the positive, engage with the positive, and post positive, I usually find that's what follows you! So influencers can be a more positive influence by being honest, fighting for good, and being kind. I think that's what we all should do to be more positive.

Q: What is your least favorite part about brand collaborations?

A: I feel like my least favorite part about social media or brand collaborations is that things can feel too salesy! It feels inauthentic. So again that's why I only like to collaborate with brands or people that I really enjoy, and that probably means that I don't make as much money with my social media as I could. But I think that my favorite part is that I can choose to engage with the people that are doing the things I support and can get behind. Sometimes brand collaborations tempt people to either go out of their genre or they tempt people with money. They think, 'Oh this looks really cool,' and then you get a lot of money, but a whole bunch of followers see that you are kind of being salesy or inauthentic and you lose a lot of your street credit.

Q: Is blogging your full-time job/source of income?

A: My husband is a full-time financial advisor, so that is our full-time job. For me, I'm doing this part-time. I am also a mom to two little kids. If not for all my busyness, I would probably share my

YouTube to a point where I would be making more. I just don't have the time right now. So maybe one day it might be, but for now it's more part-time.

Q: What is the number-one tip or piece of advice that you would give an influencer starting out?

A: I would say you never hope harder than you work! You never dream harder than you work. I believe a lot of the work has to be done on yourself first. You need to figure out what you are interested in and pursue that. Don't quit your day job before you invest and work hard to build a platform. For example: I love to garden and I also love to paint. My husband also happens to love to garden, so that's something that was already naturally built into our lives. The mint gardener was a very natural way to transition from planting in our garden, what I love to do already, combined with my passions and interests. Sharing feels very natural, and sure, sometimes social media feels like work. I show up because that's what you do for work, but it does make the job a lot more enjoyable because I am already sharing about things that I absolutely love.

Q: Number-one tips that brands are looking to engage in influencers?

A: Find influencers that are on brand and that are not posting a ton of selfies. I think that's my tip. A lot of people follow things because these are things that they are already interested in. So brands should look for influencers that are already sharing what they are interested in.

Q: What genre does your platform fall under?

A: I think it's art. Sometimes it's DIY. I think a lot of people are following me for tutorials, and I have a lot of people that just follow me because they like to see beautiful things. I have a lot of people following me that are either wanting to be watercolor artists, currently are watercolor artists, or they want to be watercolor teachers. Then you got the random person who lives in Seattle, and they are like, 'Oh you live in Seattle and you are doing fun things in Seattle. You know people I know and you just happen to create beautiful art, but it's all those things that I know and love so it feels good to look at.'

Q: Who do you like to work with and why?

A: I love working with people that are excited about what I am doing. As an artist they don't come to me with an image that I want to copy. They have a few images that they love or they have a few ideas they love and then they want to talk creatively. They might be a brand that wants to build a logo, either a garden brand on my platform or the company I work with called Good Dirt. They literally sell dirt but they want their packaging to look beautiful, engaging, and capture peoples' eye. So they just want me to create something beautiful that catches the millennials' eye! It's amazing because they started as super grassroots and got picked up for the second year at Target—and they're at Costco right now. Target told them that they picked them because of their packaging, which was just such a huge compliment to me. I designed it to be eye-catching, but it is also what I do. Then to combine it with gardening products is like a dream come true, so it just hit all the boxes.

Q: How did you find your most successful brand relationships? Did you reach out to brands or did they come to you?

A: I would say it's half and half. Most of the successful ones came to me, but sometimes the world and social media is becoming so loud that you can miss someone right under your nose. I often reject people and then change my mind, and it turns into a really wonderful relationship. It's kind of half and half, but you have to spend a lot of time on Instagram really engaging with people that you genuinely are interested in. And because of the algorithm, brands that are genuinely looking to engage will pop up—which is the benefit of the algorithms.

Q: How do you think working with influencers is different than other fields you worked in?

A: It feels a bit more authentic. A lot of people approach sharing on their Instagram like I do—especially my co-influencers. They may not have thousands and thousands of followers, but they have a few, like 5,000 or even under, but really dedicated followers. Those people show up and they buy. They may know the person intimately or they don't, or a cousin knows them and they trust their opinion. In the old world of marketing, I was an Economics major at the University of Washington. The rule of marketing was the rule of seven. Now I think with the social-media age and marketing it's like the rule of seventeen. You have to show people so many times before they even remember or recognize that they have seen it for them to actually start wanting it. Advertisements are coming at people so often that I feel like working with influencers is a better approach. I'm talking about things like replica surfaces to make these beautiful replica marble shiplap surfaces. It's a really easy-to-use material. You can put it out on your counter and all of a sudden you don't have to buy brand new marble countertops. You have one that's portable and can go anywhere. I can find really good lighting and take great, fabulous pictures. I've been sharing about them nonstop and she is not paying me, but I absolutely love what she is doing. She is so thrilled because she says people are loving what I am saying. She keeps sending me more free product, which is fabulous. So it is mutually beneficial and then more people are seeing it. They are seeing that I love it and they see that we are working together. I think this is different than a commercial or a billboard. There is a human connection behind it. That's why influencers make a real-life human influence. It's not someone being paid, like a model or an actor. It feels real, even though people usually are being modeled or paid to be an actor. It's kind of ironic!

Q: How do you measure the effectiveness of your campaigns?

A: A lot of skill. When brands want to advertise with me there are a lot of screenshots of views per story. They don't want to see any stories beyond a week. They want to see click-throughs and things like that. Sometimes the effectiveness cannot be measured in statistics. Another watercolor brand sent me so much product, and then they paid me to post. In the beginning, they weren't seeing a lot of turnaround, and I just said give it time. People have to see it a lot, they have to see me use it, they have to see me get really excited about it, and they have to see that they need it. So it's been four months and now it's really picking up. Their sales are really picking up too. Now they see what I mean. It's like you have to create the need and show the need. For me, in order to be authentic, I have to find the need. Sometimes it takes a little bit of time with a product, but with painting I can find the need in some really fabulous blue paint.

Q: Where do you feel Influencer Marketing and influencers in general are going in the next two or three years?

A: People say that Instagram is not going to be here in two to three years, but me and my friends have actually talked about it and we think that Instagram is going to become the new hub. I think it's going to be your website, and websites will become obsolete. It's street cred, because with Instagram you have a lot of followers. Having a website means you are authentic and you are a real person. That's almost like the verified check, I believe. I think that Instagram is going to be the hub of the wheel and either link tree or that one hyperlink will take you to a spot where you can access all the other platforms like YouTube, GoShare, or whatever else is coming. I don't think Instagram is going anywhere. I think it's just going to get bigger and more influential and more dynamic.

INFLUENCER SPOTLIGHT: MOOREA SEAL

Instagram: @mooreaseal

Moorea Seal is the author of 52 Lists for Happiness, The 52 Lists Project, Make Yourself at Home, and founder of mooreaseal.com.

Q: How did you become an influencer?

A: When I was six years old, I remember seeing a five-year-old painter in Russia earn $1,000,000 from selling her paintings. I realized that I was already a year older than her and that I had to make my dreams come true already. I was more motivated by ambition than money. I tend to see an opportunity, and I'm instantly motivated to seize it. I'm not afraid to fail because I see failure as an opportunity to pivot.

I graduated from college during the recession in 2009 with a degree in illustration. At the time, there were no jobs at all in Seattle, so I began blogging. I started in Xanga, then moved to LiveJournal, Friendster, and then Myspace. I used to be a musician, and I wrote an album when I was nineteen. So, Myspace was the first place I really started to inadvertently develop an online persona. I just wanted to share my stuff.

However, it dawned on me that I had six months before I had to start paying back my student loans. And, since there were no jobs, I decided that I should use my creativity to be a self-starter. I began working as an artist assistant to a sculptor in Seattle, and I realized that I wouldn't be able to sustain myself as an artist assistant for $8 an hour. So, I figured if I was able to make art and sell it, then I'd be doing something that I love while also sustaining myself. Of course, the one class that I didn't take in my art department was metalsmithing, and upon graduating I wanted to teach myself about jewelry making. It's like a mini sculpture and easy to ship. Since I was already blogging about ten times a week, I taught myself jewelry making and started my own Etsy shop. My jewelry creations had taken off in the blogging world, and by 2011, I already had forty different stores across the world wholesaling or stocking my jewelry. Since I had done well with building my community through blogging, I didn't need to reach out to anyone else.

Around the same time, I noticed that there were no templates or designs for blogs, which made them quite unattractive. So, I decided to teach myself coding and some basic HTML. I did that on LiveJournal when I was sixteen, so there was no reason I couldn't do it now at twenty-three. I applied my graphic-design and illustration skills, and I started doing freelance blog design and portraiture for bloggers. I also figured out how to create ads for people. As a result, I got picked up by a company in Canada of two women who were also starting to do blog design, and we formed the blog design team before there were blog designers.

Soon after, I started using Pinterest when it was in beta. I thought it would be a great way for me to collect and create inspiration boards for my design clients, since I would get so many emails with different images of inspiration. But I ended up working late into the night on my design projects, so to take a break, I began pinning stuff.

I had also wanted to be a museum curator in my teens, and pinning was like collecting and curating things. I was doing this before anyone was talking about curation as a thing that anybody could do. Then one day one of my sponsors for my blog, who would send me product in exchange for a post once a month (it was the very early days of Influencer Marketing, and only a few brands were starting to do this), asked me for my stats on all my different social-media sites. I had a couple thousand on my blog and a couple thousand on Twitter. But when I pulled up my Pinterest stats, which I'd only had for about six months, it was 250,000. So, I emailed Pinterest and asked if there was a glitch, since there weren't that many users. And they told me there was no glitch, that their users really loved my boards and pinning style. So, they started to promote me.

As a result, for the first three or four years of Pinterest, I was in the top five most-followed people on Pinterest. By Christmas of 2012, Pinterest did "30 Days of Pinspiration," where they featured huge celebrities and top pinners, and the only two regular people who were featured in the "30 days of Pinspiration" were me and one other blogger. Our faces were alongside Dr. Oz, Martha Stewart, Oprah, and the Army. So, I was receiving organic promotion because people were genuinely interested in following me for what I was doing.

Then an agent reached out to me. I was one of their first five influencers, and they must have been one of the first companies to build an agency around influencers. I did campaigns for Madewell, J. Crew, Anthropologie, Nordstrom, P&G, L'Oreal, home-decor companies, West Elm. I did it all. But the more clients they began taking on, the less campaigns were being offered to me, which didn't make much sense to me with my branding, voice, and authenticity—which is the norm in social media today, but it wasn't at that time.

So, in 2012, I realized that since I had a million followers on Pinterest and I was desirable as an influencer, I should be doing this for myself and I should be going direct to consumers, rather than being a voice for brands that didn't resonate with me. I realized I should be my own brand.

In fact, I had already rebranded myself at nine years old. My original name is Ashley, but I had been through some very traumatic events, and I just decided I needed to get rid of that old person. I needed to get rid of that name, and I gave myself the name Moorea. So, since I already had a huge following and a recognizable name, I partnered with my business partner who's also my cousin. He's a very self-made person as well, and we decided to open an online retail site where I curated about forty different designers who I met through Etsy and blogging. I used that network of bloggers that I had become friends with over the past three years to be my marketing. Because I genuinely cared about them and they genuinely cared about me, they were happy to talk about my stuff.

And within two weeks of launching our site, we received a cease and desist from Madewell, which was a good sign. We had a bracelet that featured a clasp function that they had trademarked. That made me realize that I had become a competitor with the people that I used to market for, and they were watching me. So over the years, as a small retailer, I saw major brands pick up unknown brands that I stocked in my store, as well as brands like Anthropologie and Urban Outfitters pick up interns who I featured in my store, like people from my small hometown.

From there, we decided to open a storefront, because our company was growing really quickly and we needed a new office. So, we got a tiny little storefront on Third Avenue in Seattle and built it out quite affordably. I had friends who were carpenters help me build things, and since I'm very crafty and creative, I designed everything. Similarly, I designed the entire website, I took all the photography, and I did all the copy. I managed that organic marketing through my friends who were 'tastemakers' (before influencers was the term).

Since I was still blogging, I wanted to create something on my blog that was free that could serve multiple functions for me as a creative person and someone trying to build a brand. So, I came up with the 52 Lists Project. I have always been a list-maker. I had a blog in 2007 that was called "Missed Lists" because I would just list things out, and that brought me peace to see evidence of myself out on paper or on a blog. So, I decided to create a once-a-week list to help prompt people into thinking, to make their own lists. For example, if you're someone who's very emotional, it gives you a very clean, simple way to get your thoughts and emotions out without getting wound up in them. And, if you're someone who has a hard time accessing your emotions, this is a very cerebral way of getting to what you need to know about yourself. Then, at the end of every prompt, there was a way for people to take action.

And then I figured out a way to build something out on my blog through coding, so that when people did their own lists, I made a printout. They could download it from the blog post itself, print it out; they could take a photo of it and put it on their blog, and then they could share it to my blog post so we could link our blog posts in the same place.

So, that was my first time really being strategic about how to get out into other people's spheres. It was the perfect fusion of my heart and what I care about, as well as a business mindset that I didn't know I had.

Then, a year later, my now editor walked into my storefront and said, "Hey, I'm from Sasquatch Books, and we really like your 52 Lists Project. We really love your voice. Have you ever thought about writing a book?" She thought that 52 Lists would make a great book.

The day my book got released, it got picked up by Anthropologie, Urban Outfitters, Paper Source, and several different retailers who I had worked with as an influencer and who were watching my store. Then, within about three months, my book ironically shot up to number fifty-two on Amazon.

My second book, *52 Lists for Happiness*, came out a year later and hit number two on all of Amazon a year after it came out. It was featured on Oprah's website and in her newsletters twelve times.

So, now I have a weird amalgamation of a million different things that I do as an entrepreneur, as a creative person, and as a person who genuinely cares about the health and safety of people. I have the storefront. I have the online site. I have my books, which I've sold over a million copies of in five years. I have a jewelry line. I have branded clothing that I've designed. I have branded desktop products. And I expect to do a whole lot more in my lifetime if I've been able to do this in just ten years.

Q: Do you hire influencers for anything now?

A: Now I don't do a ton of hiring influencers for stuff. I have quite a variety of ways that, as a retailer, I've worked with influencers over the years. It started as an organic relationship that I had with other influencers and I still have because I genuinely cared about them. The people who actually care and build real relationships are the people that win.

In the early days of blogging and before we had a name for ourselves, we were just doing it because we were creative and wanted to be bigger than the whole narrative of being a boss girl. I honestly didn't resonate with the Sophia Amoruso narrative of being a girl boss because I thought it was pretty belittling and simplistic. It's no joke to be in business. As someone who built a little business in Etsy, I knew just how hard it was to build a brand and a business without having a degree in business. And I had seen over the years the sort of manipulation that has been placed on women especially aspiring to be business owners and aspiring to be influencers. There's been a whole development of networking to that demographic.

There's a documentary on a company that shows that the world of influencers and blogging has become a world of massive pyramid schemes. They tell women that they want to empower them, that they believe in their voice. They get them to join their community to sell their stuff. I've seen huge pyramid schemes within essential oils and stay-at-home moms who are wanting to have a career as an influencer or trying to find a way to build out their own income. And many smart people in business are always looking for ways to do that. I mean, they're trying to maximize profit, and this is just one more way to do it. Now we have essential-oil parties. We have retail brands that sell clothing, and we have parties that could win you a car if you sell it in your home to your friends. That's all still happening within the influencer world, the Instagram world, the blogging world.

They're capitalizing on people's vulnerability. And, that is what I fight the hardest against. I want to use my influence for good and for protecting and empowering people because most of the people who are influencers are women. The first influencers were mostly women. Most of them were women who worked from home or who stayed at home, who had free time.

I have a lot of friends within the Mormon community who are women who I met through blogging in early 2000s because they weren't allowed by their family, their culture, their religion to be working mothers. But their way around it was to start a blog and to build a side hustle through that. It's a really interesting and beautiful story of empowerment, and women trying to find their voice, and women trying to have ownership of their own lives.

Q: Talk to me about how you're trying to make the world of influencers a more positive place for people.

A: What I've learned from doing influencer work and being a retailer over the last ten years is that, above all else, I want to be an advocate and I want to be someone who fights for people's personal wellness, which has also become an incredibly hot topic because of social media and influencers. Kids are growing up in such a different world when it comes to interacting with social media than I did. We got cell phones at the end of high school. We got Facebook our freshman year of college, when it was only accessible to college students. I was a part of the first generation of so many of these different things.

I have two younger sisters, one is nine years younger than me, and I'm observing her life that is under the influence of influencers and the sorts of pressures and expectations that everyday people now have to create a brand for themselves. With the pressure of influencers, people now feel like they must create an Instagram for their baby so that they have that lineage for when they get to when they're twenty and they want to start their own brand. We're in a crazy culture of this narrative where being an influencer is core to being a human almost. Having your brand, having your color palette, having your typography. Everything that I studied, it's fascinating to now see young people, twelve-year-olds, thirteen-year-olds hopping on Instagram and deciding that they have to create who they are, who they must present to the world so they can get deals and get free stuff, so they can build their own business someday.

Q: What's your advice to influencers and brands in this space?

A: I hope that people can use my life, my experiences, and my career path as a template of what to do and what not to do. At the end of the day, every generation is seeking safety and seeking security for themselves. And I think that the world of influencing is just another reflection of people trying to find validation for themselves, to have their voice heard, and to gain compensation for what they express, what they share, and what they pursue.

So, all of that is why I do the work that I do and what I write. And when I contemplate, I look at life from a very philosophical view and I expect that in the coming years, more people are going to feel prompted to do so as well, because the world of ethics and morals is so ambiguous and we see shifts happening through Facebook and their control of things, for example. I think that there's going to be a lot more debate around ethics and morality when it comes to influencing and transparency. And, the best thing to do is to still pursue being truthfully yourself, even when you are afraid as an influencer that it will lose you money. Things are going to keep changing. I mean, the thing that you've done so beautifully is the thing you've done because you wanted to.

INFLUENCER SPOTLIGHT: MORGAN HALEY

Instagram: @FindingMorganTyler, previously @the_southern_ yogi

Morgan Haley is an influential figure in the health and wellness space, specializing in her yoga practice, where she reaches an Instagram audience of nearly 500,000 followers. She's been through the ups and downs of what it means to be a social-media influencer and a small-business owner.

Q: Did you ever set out to become an influencer?

A: You know, I never, ever in a million years thought I'd be a social-media 'influencer.' When I first hopped on IG, it was just for fun—like everyone else. I was working in my field as a vascular sonographer and then switched over to being a barista so I could focus more on yoga. Once I started posting snippets of my yoga journey, my account blew up. Like, went from two hundred followers to 100,000 in under a year. That's when brands started reaching out to me, people wanting to pay me for posts. I was both flattered and shocked. This began my journey of making Instagram my full-time job. It kind of fell straight into my lap.

Q: Have you ever experienced any of the negative side-effects of social media?

A: Oh, absolutely. Every choice you make is scrutinized by thousands of people. It's a bit crippling at times. I've had death threats made, hate-mail sent, and even people spying on me at local restaurants and gyms only to report my every move to troll accounts. It used to make me want to never post again. But over the years I've learned you can only feel sad for those people, and the lives they must lead have led them to target so much hate towards someone they don't even know.

Q: What piece of advice would you give to brands?

A: Stop sending mass emails out. We know when you've sent the same email to hundreds of other influencers. It definitely doesn't make us feel special or that you 'really loved our page.' Personal emails and attention to details go a long way.

Q: Do you have an example of a collaboration with a brand that went poorly?

A: I collaborated with a major mall clothing store once for an activewear campaign. Somewhere along the way there was a miscommunication, and weeks after I'd posted this campaign for them, they noticed I hadn't added one specific word to my caption. They wanted me to redo the entire campaign. I felt a bit taken advantage of, as it wasn't noticed immediately, and the ads had been up on my page for a while, giving them massive amounts of exposure. Now they wanted me to do it all again. I refused, and then they refused to send the winners of my giveaway posts their gift cards. So not only did I not get paid for that campaign, but I had to purchase the gift cards myself and mail them out.

Q: What are your thoughts on how influencing impacts daily life?

A: I think it's only negatively increased the comparison game, and comparison is the thief of joy. People are looking at others' homes, relationships, bodies, and just lifestyles in general and wondering if they could do better. No one waters their own grass anymore, and everyone yearns for their neighbor's instead. The grass is greener where you water it! On the flip side—I think it's allowed so many people our age to completely thrive with entrepreneurship and small businesses. It's created a community where you aren't simply limited to a brick and mortar clientele, but can offer your passions and business to people globally with the click of a button.

Q: What is your least favorite part of working with brands?

A: I'd say the rules. Ha-ha. I hate complying with contractual obligations. Every brand or company has something they want you to do or say—whether it's specific wording or verbiage, or how a photo looks that isn't quite 100 percent authentic to you and your page.

Q: Is blogging your full-time job?

A: I'm not so much a blogger (in the writing sense) as an instructor and lifestyle influencer. I make my living selling my yoga videos on a subscription-based app, and also selling my personal merchandise like face masks, scrunchies, headbands and ball caps on my website. But yes—Instagram, and all it entails, is my full-time gig!

APPENDIX F
BRAND SPOTLIGHTS

Portions of these spotlights appear throughout the book. The entire transcript is included in this appendix.

BRAND SPOTLIGHT: WYLDE LINGERIE

www.wyldelingerie.com

Instagram: @wyldelingerie

About Wylde Lingerie

Wylde is a Seattle-based, women-owned lingerie brand born out of love for lingerie and all things romantic. Their intimates bring together a touch of love, lust, and romance, and their mission is to celebrate women by providing an intimate layer for self-expression while cultivating femininity and empowerment. They believe in enhancing a woman's body without the need to change anything, and think of their pieces as love potions, for self love and all other loves.

An interview with co-founders Vera Burgos and Romina Serrate

Q: What percentage of your marketing budget/energy goes into Influencer Marketing compared to your other forms of marketing?

A: About 35 percent.

Q: Share an example of a recent campaign that went well.

A: We partnered up with ten influencers for our latest summer capsule. Each influencer produced content showcasing our new pieces to be featured in our Instagram page. The content we received was unique. Each influencer created what they felt would resonate with their audience, and we loved that variety. The creative freedom allows for the content to feel authentic. It also encourages our customers to have fun and tap into their artistic side to post their pictures with our product to be featured too.

Q: How do you measure campaign success?

A: We mostly measure success by tracking key performance indicators like influencer promo codes, email sign-ups, reach, impressions, engagement, and website traffic.

Q: What do you look for in an influencer partnership?

A: Brand awareness. Influencers spend lots of time and effort building their follower base who trust them and the recommendations they make. It's a vote of confidence.

Q: How do you vet influencers to ensure success?

A: We look at the overall effort they've put into their own personal branding and previous content they have created—the latter to ensure that they are a good match for our brand values. We also love good storytellers.

Q: What characteristics of influencers do you look for (size, brand, demographics, style, etc.)?

A: We try to incorporate different types of influencers as much as we can. We celebrate diversity and work with a mix of micro and macro influencers. At the same time, each campaign might require different characteristics depending on the goals we are looking to achieve. Our upcoming campaign, for example, taps on local Seattle influencers.

Q: Can you think of a campaign that was unsuccessful or a bad experience?

A: Our first influencer campaign was a learning experience in that out of fifteen influencers we chose to work with for the product release, two didn't deliver. From this we learned how to better assess the influencers we partner with. Now we also intentionally schedule a few exchanges with them prior to the agreement to get a feel for their level of commitment. It doesn't mean that it won't happen again, but we are taking measures to ensure that we can improve and continue to build meaningful partnerships.

Q: What are the difficulties of working with influencers?

A: We are a small business so our partnerships with influencers are often personal, and there is room for flexibility. Because we don't work with more than ten to fifteen influencers at a time, we can easily keep track of deliverables. I would think that larger campaigns could get more complex and would require an implementation of some sort of workflow or process to ensure that deployment dates are on target with other marketing efforts, etc.

Q: What are the pluses of working with influencers?

A: Access to their audience—and it's not the same as their audience seeing a paid ad for your brand. This is the influencer personally recommending your product, which adds credibility to the brand. We've also come across other great business opportunities through influencers.

Q: Where do you see Influencer Marketing going in the next year or two?

A: Social media continues to deeply influence consumer behavior, and I don't see that changing any time soon. Most influencers vet the brands that they work with so that they can continue to add value for their followers. There's an added layer of transparency that gives their supporters more confidence when making purchase decisions. The reliance on influencers continues to grow while trust for traditional ads decreases.

Q: How do you find influencers? Do you use any Influencer Marketing platforms or agencies?

A: We do not use any platforms or third-party agencies. We tracked down influencers that were a good match for our desired brand's voice for our first campaign. Since then, we have continued to work with some of the same influencers and others that were referred to us by them. We also often receive influencer package offers via email.

Q: What social channels do you prefer and why?

A: Instagram has proven to be the most successful for us. I think that is because it's highly visual, and that's great for branding. We are hoping to tap into YouTube next year, mostly because we want to get more trustworthy reviews that instill confidence in those who are interested in purchasing from our brand.

Q: What are the primary benefits you receive from campaigns (e.g. photos, exposure, sales, affiliation with an influential person, etc.)? A: Content and brand awareness. Content is costly to produce, and branding takes time. Influencer Marketing helps us with both of these.

Q: Do you require ownership of copyright for content?

A: Yes, it is part of our influencer agreement.

Q: What advice would you give influencers who wish to be on PR lists?

A: To build a strong online presence with high quality, regularly published content. Companies like to see that you are dedicated. Once you have this, identify brands that you honestly love and can relate to. We personally love to work with influencers who send us messages about how much they love our product or how beautiful and confident they felt while producing content for us.

Q: What do you look for in an influencer PR kit?

A: Audience insight, links, and references to past works. It also helps if they have a list of their offerings and if they specialize in other channels for consideration in future campaigns.

Q: What components of the contract are most important to you?

A: The roles and delivery requirements need to be defined for each party, as well as the terms of the working relationship. Having these in place from the beginning help set a clear communication path moving forward.

Q: How do you go about creating a campaign (do you let the influencer run with it, do you have a team that creates the concepts, etc.)?

A: Once we have chosen who to work with, we trust their creative process. A good influencer knows what resonates best with their audience. This circles back to the influencers knowing who follows them, and consistency of posting and content on their feeds.

Q: What is the most important key to success in Influencer Marketing in your opinion?

A: To focus on choosing the right influencers for a campaign. They will be the face of the brand, so it is important that their values are in sync, in my opinion.

Q: What about your brand is attractive to influencers? What could make your brand more attractive?

A: We strive to connect our product with a purpose, which is for our lingerie to be the layer of confidence that enhances and empowers the feminine in every woman. We hope that this combination is what attracts influencers to work with us.

Q: How do you feel about influencers purchasing followers? What about influencers who have used advertising to grow their audience?

A: It seems to me that the purpose of being an influencer is to create and nourish a relationship with an audience, and if they are purchasing followers, that isn't happening. Advertising through cost per click, for example, is a whole different ball game. If you produced great content and want to reach a larger audience, paid advertising is a great idea. At that point you are not paying for followers, you are paying for exposure and users will choose to follow you or not depending on whether your content aligns with them.

Q: Are you seeing any new platforms emerging that people should be paying attention to?

A: Social media seems to be changing constantly, and as new platforms emerge it is important to keep your target audience in mind. There's a lot of buzz around TikTok right now, especially if your target audience is Gen Z users.

Q: Anything else we should include to help brands and influencers achieve more success with Influencer Marketing?

A: There is a good side and a bad side to almost everything. But in our experience, this strategy can be beneficial for the brand, the influencer, and the consumer. When done right, these relationships can be genuine and not just paid transactional exchanges. If we can keep them this way, Influencer Marketing can play a role in encouraging brands to do their due diligence to be transparent and intentional about their practices. Influencers are able to profit from supporting and creating content for products/services they are passionate about, and the consumer gets honest, trustworthy reviews.

BRAND SPOTLIGHT: BUKI

www.bukibrand.com
Instagram: @bukibrand

About Buki

Buki (boo-key) is a Seattle-based brand that specializes in luxury clothing sustainably crafted with state-of-the-art Japanese fiber technology, fabulous fits, and travel-ready comfort. Buki was co-founded by the husband-wife team of designer/entrepreneur Joey Rodolfo and marketer Stacy Bennett. Their men's and women's collections are exclusively crafted with their range of proprietary technical fabrics that provide fabrics that thermo-regulate to their collagen fabric, which softens and hydrates the skin. Buki is the Japanese word for "defend and protect," which is in reference to what the technical fabrics do for the wearer. The company is on trend with the rise of "ath-leisure" and "ath-lifestyle" clothing, as well as Wearable Wellness.

An interview with Stacy Bennett, co-founder and COO of Buki

Q: Do you work with influencers?

A: Yes, we do. In fact, we launched the brand with an influencer program. We focused on local micro-influencers and it definitely helped drive brand awareness.

Q: What analytics tools do you use?

A: We love analytics and use Shopify analytics, Google analytics, Facebook analytics, Instagram analytics, and retail store specific analytics through Square.

Q: What do you look for in an influencer partnership?

A: We believe in win-win partnerships, where each party receives something of value. On our side, we look for great content that reflects the brand and tells our story in a photo. For the influencer, we look to provide a way for them to be an opinion leader and receive clothing as a thank-you for the partnership. We have several influencers that consistently deliver value for us, and we try to work with them as often as possible.

Q: How do you vet influencers to ensure success?

A: When looking at a new influencer that we haven't worked with before, I look for several key variables: Are they authentic and genuine? Are they reflecting their unique story in an authentic and genuine way? Then, I look at their audience size, but more importantly their engagement rate. Once those are a green light, I lay out the expectations clearly—from the look/feel/mood we're going for, to the timeline that we need the content to be delivered. Ninety percent of the time, everything goes smoothly. Once we find an influencer that is great to work with and they consistently deliver value, we build the relationship into an ongoing partnership.

Q: What characteristics of influencers do you look for (size, brand, demographics, style, etc.)?

A: We look at their audience size, engagement, if their look/feel/style/story is a fit with ours, and if their audience is consistent with ours.

Q: Can you share a story about an unsuccessful or negative experience with influencers?

A: Early into launching our brand, we worked with an influencer who provided us with her photos. We used them in our social content and a store marketing piece. We were contacted by the influencer's photographer, who insisted that those photos were her property and that we stop using them immediately. I reached out to the influencer to ask about it and she was taken aback as well. We discontinued using the photos and haven't worked with that influencer again either. I'm a big believer in giving credit where credit is due, and gave the photographer credit in the one to two uses of the photos. So in an abundance of caution, we simply stopped using the photos and didn't work with the influencer or the photographer again.

Q: What are the difficulties of working with influencers?

A: I've had an agreement with an influencer, sent them product, and they have never delivered content. They stop responding as well. It's not a good way of doing business, but it has happened to us a couple of times. It is the exception, not the rule, however.

Q: How do you find influencers? Do you use any Influencer Marketing platforms or agencies?

A: Because we are a startup with a small team, I rely on good, old-fashioned prospecting on IG. If I see someone that would be a good fit I reach out with a DM, or influencers will reach out to us via DM or EM. I haven't used any platforms or agencies—I think with a bigger program, those would have value, but for where we are now, it's working well.

Q: Do you offer PR packages and gifts for influencer content, or do you prefer to use paid/sponsored ad content?

A: Because we are a startup, we predominantly leverage PR packages of clothing gifts in exchange for influencer content. That mostly limits us to small, micro-influencers, but the current trend is with micro-influencers because they are more believable. Plus, you never know who is going to hit it big. Early on when I ran Clarisonic's digital-marketing program, I did a product trade with a small influencer (they were called bloggers back then) who did a video review in exchange for the gifted Clarisonic—she turned out to be Michelle Phan, who, of course, went on to become huge, and she launched her own cosmetics company with L'Oréal.

Q: Are you seeing any new platforms emerging that people should be paying attention to?

A: LinkedIn seems to be the newest platform to pay attention to. They've done a good job of transforming their platform from a networking site only to a content distribution network.

BRAND SPOTLIGHT: NATURA CULINA

Instagram: @naturaculina

About Natura Culina

Natura Culina is a wellness skincare brand promoting green and sustainable products and practices.

An interview with Natura Culina

Q: Do you work with influencers?

A: Yes. We have brand ambassadors, and we are constantly striving to collaborate with social media influencers.

Q: What percentage of your marketing budget/energy goes into Influencer Marketing?

A: It takes a big chunk of our time-schedule to plan and coordinate. I would say about 30 percent. As far as marketing costs, our ambassadors make a percentage of each sale with their ambassador code or influencer link.

Q: What is an example of a recent campaign that went well?

A: A recent campaign that was successful was a collaboration with our ambassador and product partner Morgan Tyler. Morgan hosted a "NC Day" on her page that resulted in her offering the following promotion—spend forty-five dollars and receive a free Rose'Berry Face Mask with your order when you apply code "roseberry" to your card. This campaign proved to be very successful.

Q: How do you vet influencers to ensure success?

A: We exercise a trial period with our influencers. We choose influencers who have a genuine connection to Natura Culina so that they are transparent when promoting our brand. We send each individual our product to sample before offering them an opportunity to become one of our influencers. If they take to our products and want to join our team, we give them an influencer code or affiliate link to track their promotions and reward them through a commission on each sale.

Q: What are the benefits of working with influencers?

A: Influencers have a way of telling their version of the story that your brand represents. It's beautiful to see how each person takes to NC and how the brand has heightened and changed their lives. People get to see NC through each influencer's lens.

Q: Have you experienced a negative collaboration?

A: Yes, there is one collaboration where we received pushback. We collaborated with a small, woman-owned business that made handmade leather bags. Our vegan/cruelty-free followers did not support the idea of us promoting a company that sells leather goods. We learned that we have to be very careful and consider all angles of each collaboration.

BRAND SPOTLIGHT: THE MODERN NURSERY

www.plantsbypost.com

*Instagram: @_plantsbypost_*

About The Modern Nursery

As third-generation greenhouse growers in Northern California, the Modern Nursery is committed to delivering products with principles that have always been at the root of their family owned and operated business—to grow the best selection of plants with quality always striving to be better.

An interview with Andi, Digital Marketing Coordinator

Q: How do you measure campaign success?

A: We're a very small team, so the success of a campaign isn't necessarily about making more sales, although that is a plus. We're mostly focused on exposure right now, with attempting to gain real followers that stay with us.

Q: What analytics tools do you use?

A: We use Instagram's analytics, as well as Planoly for planning posts and assessing engagement analytics.

Q: What do you look for in an influencer partnership?

A: There are so many things to look for in an influencer partnership. We focus on an alignment of interest and product—for example, if the influencer knows of us or posts about plants in general; how our products fit into their lifestyle and business; and if our product organically fits into their feed, versus feeling forced. We also prioritize how well we can get along with the influencer. In a world of constant communication and exposure, it's important to us here to associate with kind, thoughtful, and aware individuals.

Q: What characteristics of influencers do you look for?

A: Style and brand are the most important categories for us when it comes to looking for influencers.

Q: What are the difficulties of working with influencers?

A: Timely communication is the biggest challenge. Both parties are usually quite busy with their own work, so managing to coordinate time can be difficult. It's always a good idea to start as early as possible when planning a collaboration.

Q: What about the pluses?

A: Gaining exposure to a lot of people that otherwise wouldn't have heard of us is a huge plus. Another plus is that we're given the chance to build a relationship with each influencer. We consider it no different than networking, which helps to ensure that we'll have more opportunities to work with the influencer again in the future.

Q: What are the titles of the people who work with influencers at your company, and are they responsible for other duties?

A: I, Andi, am our digital-marketing coordinator and Sami is in charge of purchasing, as well as supervisor/general manager of our small team. Both Sami and I have many responsibilities, which is likely the reason Influencer Marketing hasn't been a top priority at the moment.

Q: How large is your Influencer Marketing team?

A: There are just two of us.

Q: What social channels do you prefer and why?

A: We mostly use Instagram at the moment, given our capacity. I really like that Instagram allows the user to plan posts ahead of time, which is helpful when there is a lot of other work to focus on.

Q: What are the primary benefits you receive from campaigns?

A: Primarily, the photos we get, the vast exposure, and the resulting sales.

Q: How do you go about creating a campaign?

A: Typically Sami and I discuss a high-level strategy, then we present it to the influencer and give them room to be creative and make suggestions.

Q: Any final thoughts?

A: Influencers are more than just a follower count. The future needs to trend toward building a more personal connection to those in our social-media endeavors. Find influencers that align with your values and beliefs, communicate well with them, treat them kindly, and always be open to compromise. I've witnessed some great opportunities fall through because of poor treatment and absurd expectations.

BRAND SPOTLIGHT: OUTREACH

www.outreach.io

About Outreach

Outreach uses up-and-coming individuals to model their software to the public. From social events to conventions and trade shows, influencers are helping drive traffic and sales for business assets. The term influencer hasn't quite reached this market but that isn't holding them back! They are forging the way and helping reform how we think of influence.

An interview with Max Altschuler, vice president of marketing at Outreach

Q: Who is your perfect influencer and how are you reaching them?

A: LinkedIn is like the Instagram of business. As companies change how we reach our customers, we are seeing a shift in how each platform is used. LinkedIn provides a place to teach a potential client as well as build a relationship and foundation that encourages organic sales and growth. With the knowledge of our ideal customer, we can reach out to people as potential influencers. We have dialed in the best size of a person or company to invest our influencer budget in, and where they are in their career. We know we want them to be up-and-coming and provide equal amounts of give and take. Since we know who our ideal influencer is, we can hone in on those metrics as we build relationships.

Q: Do you use contracts, and what specifics do you have your Influencers sign?

A: When Outreach.io starts a new relationship with an influencer, it isn't taken lightly. We are proactive in learning not only about the business but also the personal life of their influencers. We see the red flags and possible issues and make sure to avoid situations that can be troublesome for both parties. Outreach.io also has a thorough contract that allows space redirection in case of misconduct. We also protect our exclusivity. When contracts are signed, they are based on a one-year time frame, allowing both parties to reassess growth and needs in smaller increments of time. While business marketing plans used to span five to ten years, we are seeing a shift to smaller time frames so that there is flexibility and movement to make sure all needs are met.

Q: How are you tracking the worth of you Influencers?

A: The matrix for seeing the worth of our influencer programs is slightly different for business-to-business arrangements. While a traditional influencer arrangement may focus on impressions and sales, Outreach.io focuses on lead generation and people moving through our internal pipeline. Maybe a client who fizzled out is rejuvenated, or maybe there is a net new client who comes out of an event. Our focus is slightly different, but in the end it is still about growth and getting your name out there.

Q: What kind of strategies are you using to protect and ensure growth for your company?

A: We are aware that protecting our company and our 140,000-plus sales professionals is very important. So as we work with influencers, we have some firewalls in place. First, we make sure all contracts have a capped budget increase as well as a non-compete aspect. Second, we plan our influencers by geography of growth and as part of our big-picture marketing plan, each aspect works together with the others. Outreach.io also focuses on both companies so we are prospecting and nurturing our current clients. As a startup we know the importance of growth and how that can change our overall strategy, but we also see this with our influencers. We want to see the people and companies we work with grow, but also know that means that contracts may need to be adjusted, and some influencers may need to be let go so that they can continue their own personal path. That is one of the main reasons our marketing plan is restructured yearly and assessed often.

BRAND SPOTLIGHT: PYNE & SMITH CLOTHIERS

www.pyneandsmith.com

Instagram: @pyneandsmithclothiers

An interview with owner Joanna McCartney

Q: What do you look for in an influencer partnership?

A: Good photography, authentic messages, engaged followers, and ethics.

Q: How do you vet influencers to ensure success?

A: I review their social media posts and comments, look at their style and photography, and go from there to see if they are the right fit for our brand.

Q: What characteristics of influencers do you look for (size, brand, demographics, style, etc.)?

A: Usually engagement with their followers takes priority. I usually try to work with influencers that have at least 10,000 followers, but if they have a good message, high engagement with their audience, or really great photos, then I will also consider working with them.

Q: Can you share an example of a negative experience with a campaign?

A: I am pretty picky with influencers, so I haven't had many unsuccessful or bad experiences. But I did work with one influencer (two years ago) who I realized had bought her followers and didn't really seem genuine or care about the product. It taught me to really review their posts and who they work with before I commit to working with influencers.

Q: What social channels do you prefer and why?

Instagram and Pinterest. I find that strong imagery can help sell out dresses, so I work on these two platforms as much as possible.

ABOUT THE AUTHORS

Justin R. Blaney DM is the #1 bestselling author of fifteen books. He is followed by more than one million on Facebook and Instagram @justinblaney. He also publishes an app that features his writing, which can be found at www.justinblaney.com/app. Justin has been using, writing, and speaking about social media since 2006. His course on Influencer Marketing at University of Washington Foster School of Business is believed to be the first on the topic.

Kate Fleming is a technical marketing specialist and has spent the greater part of the last decade working as a digital analytics engineer specializing in data design and implementation. In 2018 Kate put her knowledge of data and marketing analysis to the ultimate test and launched a social profile (@the.skincare.diary) supporting her interest and fascination in skincare. She is the author of the self-published ebook *The Skincare Diary Vol I*, a self-help skincare book, and is the creator of the TSKD product line. In early 2019 Kate was named rising influencer of the year at the CEW awards in New York. She currently resides in Seattle where she continues to work in tech, run The Skincare Diary, and is now pursuing a commercial pilot certificate.